MOTHMAN

THE FACTS BEHIND THE LEGEND

MOTHMAN
THE FACTS BEHIND THE LEGEND

Donnie Sergent, Jr. & Jeff Wamsley

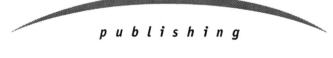

mark s. phillips
publishing
Proctorville, Ohio

Library of Congress Control Number: 2001119432
ISBN-13: 978-09667246-7-7
ISBN-10: 0-9667246-7-4

Published previously by *Mothman Lives Publishing*

Printed in the United States of America

First Edition

mark s. phillips
publishing

www.marksphillips.com

Table of Contents

Preface

This book is a documentary of the Mothman phenomenon, spanning past and present. The interviews and clippings in this book have never before been published in a documentary. To say this book was exciting to work on would be an understatement for me. The website is a lot of fun, as well. Through the Mothmanlives.com website, and my collaboration with Will Patton concerning his role in the 2002 "Mothman" movie from Sony Pictures, I've become acquainted with some very kind and interesting people I would have otherwise never come to know.

To find out more about Mothman and related subjects around Point Pleasant, please review the "Additional Resources" section I have compiled at the back of this book. You will find many sources of information to assist in discovering the truth about Mothman for yourself.

— *Donnie Sergent, Jr.*

Introduction

Although the Mothman legacy began over 40 years ago on a chilly, fall night in 1966, it has since become the stuff legends are made of. It has grown into a phenomenon known all over the world by millions of curious people asking questions: *What really happened? What did these people see? Has it been seen since?* Nothing has sparked the world's imagination and curiosity as has the mystery behind Point Pleasant, West Virginia's Mothman.

It's no secret that the Mothman legend has been, and always will be, a part of the small town of Point Pleasant. Mothman "search parties," armed with rifles and searchlights, were social gatherings for residents in the months following the very first Mothman sighting in November of 1966.

Even though I was only five years old at the time, I remember the stories told by my mother. My father worked as a full-time officer in the National Guard Armory which, at the time of the sightings, was located within what locals refer to as the "TNT area." Cars lined up for miles and patrolled the TNT area in hopes of catching a glimpse or quick sighting of the Mothman—"the big bird," as some called it.

News crews from around the world flocked to Thirtieth Street—my family's street—in upper Point Pleasant to get the scoop on the creature. The reporters hoped to be the first to get to talk to Linda Scarberry and the others who first sighted it. We lived four houses up from where Linda's parents once lived and, from what I have been told, it was a media circus with everyone trying to get the exclusive story on Mothman.

Curiosity about the Mothman has grown since the story first appeared. By passing down from generation to generation, the story has evolved into "folklore" that seems to get bigger as the years flow by. It seems as though everyone has a Mothman story or experience to tell about. By now, many have come to ask, "What is the *real* story behind the Mothman legend?"

During (and just after) the Mothman incidents, hundreds of UFO sightings in Point Pleasant and the surrounding tri-county area were reported by residents. They claimed to have seen strange, bright lights and unexplainable flying objects in the skies. Many believe that it's not a coincidence that the Mothman and UFO sightings were reported so close together and in the same relative areas.

Was it just paranoia or was there really something in the skies? The UFO reports were obviously too numerous to ignore, with reports appearing daily in the local papers as the press clippings in this book illustrate—judge for yourself.

In October, 2000, Donnie Sergent, Jr., and I were discussing the Mothman legacy. We were planning some new designs and ideas for the Mothman merchandise carried at Criminal Records, the independent record store chain I founded in 1989. It seemed as if we were being asked almost daily in our Point Pleasant location about Mothman by many customers, both local and visiting out-of-towners. Many of these questions were about the location of TNT area. Still others asked: *Did we know anyone who actually saw the Mothman?* (The answer is yes.) *What did it look like? Was it still around today?*

I thought about having Donnie create a website designed to basically answer questions and provide information about the Mothman legend. A few days later, I picked up the phone, called Donnie, and ran the idea by him for such a website (he is a website developer, with his own web solutions business.) An hour later Donnie called back and told me how he had our

"Mothman Lives" website already up and running (www.mothmanlives.com). Within days, the site had attracted thousands of curious visitors from all over the world. We knew at that moment the Mothman legend was bigger than ever.

This book is strictly a documentary presentation about the Mothman sightings and facts about Point Pleasant, West Virginia. Its contents are the product of extensive research and hours of hard work and planning. We decided from day one that this project would contain factual information and nothing contrived or embellished.

Was there such a thing as Mothman? You can decide based upon what we present in this book. We are not interested in convincing anyone that Mothman is either real *or* a hoax. In any case, we present unique press clippings and documents, exclusive interviews, and firsthand reports from those who claim to have seen the creature—plus lots of other extremely rare findings that all have an integral part in explaining what really spawned the Mothman phenomenon.

— *Jeff Wamsley*

For the hard-working people of Point Pleasant, West Virginia

PART I
HISTORICAL PERSPECTIVE

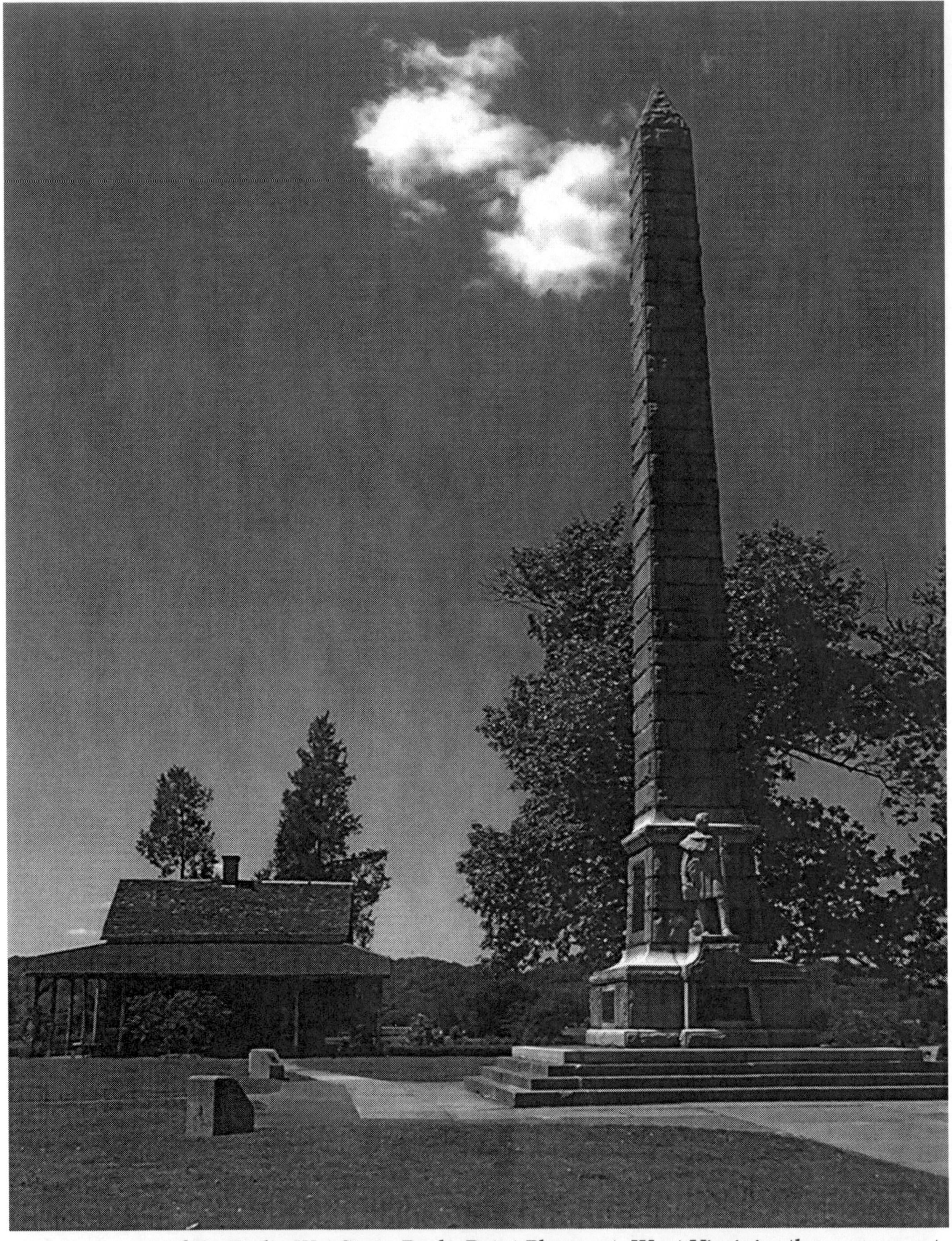

In this picture of Tu-Endie-Wei State Park, Point Pleasant, West Virginia, the monument appears to tilt due to camera lens distortion. (Photo courtesy Mark S. Phillips.)

Chapter 1: A Brief History of Mason County, WV

Mason County, West Virginia, was formed in 1804 from parts of Kanawha County and named for George Mason, author of the Constitution of Virginia and a member of the convention that framed the Constitution of the United States. This county comprised part of the proposed colony of Vandalia, the capital of which was to be Point Pleasant. Among the earliest visitors to the area were LaSalle in 1669 and Washington in 1770.

The leading industrial and agricultural products are electric power, coal, polyester resins, plastic film, flame retardant plasterizers, synthetic hydraulic fluids and lubricants, salt, hay, grain, tobacco, livestock, dairy products, poultry, fruit and vegetables.

Point Pleasant, the county seat, was named for Camp Point Pleasant, established by General Andrew Lewis in 1774. Located at the confluence of the Ohio and Kanawha Rivers, this is where Lewis and his men fought Chief Cornstalk during Lord Dunmore's War. This was the bloodiest battle ever fought between the Indians and white settlers and many claim this to be the first battle of the American Revolution. Tu-Endie-Wei State Park is the burial ground of Chief Cornstalk and frontierswoman "Mad" Ann Bailey.[1]

The Battle of Point Pleasant, West Virginia

At the confluence of the Kanawha and Ohio Rivers, the bloody, daylong Battle of Point Pleasant, West Virginia was fought. On October 10, 1774, Colonel Andrew Lewis' 1,100 Virginia

1. From official West Virginia website source: http://www.callwva.com

militiamen decisively defeated a like number of Indians lead by Shawnee Chieftain Cornstalk. Considered a landmark of frontier history, the battle is considered by some to be the first of the American Revolution. This action broke the power of the ancient Americans in the Ohio Valley and quelled a general Indian war in the frontier. Significantly, it also prevented an alliance between the British and the Indians, one which could have caused the Revolution to have a very different outcome, altering the entire history of the United States. In addition, the ensuing peace with the Indians enabled western Virginians to return across the Allegheny Mountains to aid revolutionary forces.

When Lord Dunmore (John Murray) was appointed governor of Virginia in 1771, he was ordered to discourage settlement of the lands beyond the mountains to the west. This action was motivated in part by the British government's desire to pacify the Indians by preventing encroachment on their hunting grounds and partly to preserve a profitable fur trade with the Ohio Valley tribes.

The westward migration proved difficult to halt when more and more restless settlers poured over the Alleghenies. The continued invasion aroused the native population. Their anger turned into bloody warfare early in 1774 when a group of settlers murdered the entire family of Logan, a friendly Mingo chief. Logan was so enraged that he led his tribe on the warpath, he himself taking 30 white scalps and prisoners in revenge.

Unfortunate clashes between the encroaching pioneers and the Indians continued with increasing frequency and savagery. Both groups were guilty of unthinkable atrocities, including murder, kidnaping, and infanticide.

Lord Dunmore ordered the border militia organized. Colonel Andrew Lewis, a veteran of the French and Indian Wars, was appointed commander of the Virginia troops. By carrying the fight to the Indians, Dunmore, a Tory, hoped to divert Virginians from the trouble brewing in England.

In September 1774, Dunmore signed peace treaties with the Delaware and Six Nations of the Iroquois at Pittsburgh. He then started down the Ohio River to give battle to the fierce Shawnee. Under Cornstalk, the Shawnee tribe had allied itself with Logan's Mingo to turn the frontier "red with Long Knives' blood." Meanwhile, Lewis' army had marched from Fort Union (Lewisburg) to the point of the confluence of the Great Kanawha and Ohio Rivers. He then established camp to await Dunmore's arrival from the north.

This pincer movement was thwarted when Cornstalk abandoned his Ohio River Villages north of Point Pleasant before Dunmore's forces arrived. He then attacked Lewis while the white forces were still divided, and they engaged in a bloody battle characterized by a succession of individual hand-to-hand combats. Fought on this point of land known by the Wyandotte Indian phrase "tu-endie-wei," or "the point between two waters," the battle raged all day. At times Cornstalk and his braves held the upper hand, but eventually the firepower of the backwoodsmen proved superior on the then-heavily-forested battlefield. At the end, 230 Indians were killed or wounded and more than 50 Virginians had lost their lives, including Colonel Charles Lewis, brother of the commanding officer.

Some say that before Chief Cornstalk died, he uttered a curse, a curse for the immediate area (Point Pleasant) to be stricken with hard times and sorrow for what they had done to his people. The curse was rumored to last 200 years. This cannot be confirmed, for there are no documents recording these words, but many locals hold it as truth. Some believe the Mothman is a part of that curse.

Fort Randolph

Fort Randolph at Krodel Park in Point Pleasant, West Virginia, was officially dedicated by West Virginia Governor Arch A. Moore on October 10, 1974. This was the 200th anniversary of the Battle of Point Pleasant. Fort Randolph is a large wooden replica of the fort built after the battle at the point where the Ohio and Great Kanawha Rivers meet. Built on the site of the earlier Fort Blair, Fort Randolph was a well-known outpost throughout the colonies and stood to prevent attacks on the colonies from the West during the first three years of the American Revolution. It also played a significant role in preventing an Indian Alliance with the British during the American Revolution.

The Silver Bridge Disaster

The Silver Bridge, a state-of-the-art suspension bridge, was built in 1927 spanning the Ohio River. It connected the cities of Point Pleasant, West Virginia and Gallipolis, Ohio. A new type of high- carbon steel was developed and used for the construction of the bridge. The premise for the design of the bridge was an “eyebar” suspension chain.

The bridge collapsed in December of 1967. It was toward late evening and the weather looked like snow was about to fall. Thirty-seven cars and trucks fell into the river. It was the worst road bridge disaster in U.S. history. The United States Army pulled forty-four bodies from the river; two other victims were never found.

At first, it was thought that a river barge had collided with one of the bridge supports. Another theory was that the weight of the holiday traffic had caused the collapse, due to so many vehicles on the bridge at the same time.

A government investigator, who was also a metals expert, was called in to examine the remains of the bridge which had been pulled from the river by the Army Corps of Engineers. The investigator immediately spotted something suspicious. One of the eyebars was broken in two at the circular eye. It took a massive search by a team of Army divers to recover the other half of the circular eye.

When the investigator studied the new-found piece of the eyebar, he determined that there had been a flaw in the eyebar from the day it was forged in 1926—a pre-existing crack in the eye itself. This flaw resulted in the failure of the eye years later. The weather had gradually deteriorated the steel, widening the crack in the eye, weakening it to the point of breaking. When the single eye of the link failed, it caused a chain reaction. The weight of the bridge was too much for the link on the opposite side of the bridge to bear. Within seconds, the mighty Silver Bridge collapsed in a domino-effect fashion, taking cars, trucks and passengers with it. The Silver Bridge had stood for forty-one years.

The fall of the Silver Bridge prompted the United States government to created a National Bridge Inspection Program. This program paid particular attention to bridges constructed of the same high-strength steel as the Silver Bridge in the 1920s. The new Silver Memorial Bridge now stands a short distance away from the original location of the Silver Bridge.

My mother and her mother made it safely back across the Silver Bridge into Point Pleasant just ten minutes before it collapsed. They had been in Ohio looking for a Christmas tree.

My father was working at a local lumber company in Point Pleasant when the bridge fell. He and a coworker rounded the corner of a street a couple hundred yards from the bridge. My father's co-worker said, "Oh my God, Donnie, the bridge is gone." They sat transfixed in their car as they looked at the empty space where the bridge had stood just minutes before. My father told me there were cars scattered on the streets with doors wide open; people running toward the fallen bridge.

This was a sad time in our area and my heart goes out to all family and friends of those who were affected by the collapse.

— Donnie Sergent, Jr.

The North Power Plant, where the first Mothman sighting occurred, was demolished in the early 1990s. (Photograph ©1986, courtesy Mark S. Phillips.)

Chapter 2: A History of the TNT Area

The McClintic Wildlife Area, also known to locals as the TNT area, was the backdrop of the first reported Mothman Sightings in Point Pleasant, West Virginia. It has since been a place of mystery and intrigue. The area is currently a state-owned Wildlife Management Area (WMA) and set up for public hunting, fishing and camping. It is open to the general public for all to enjoy. So, if you visit, be sure to bring your fishing poles. (I had to get that comment in for the folks at the WMA Office. I made them a promise.)

I have fished in the TNT Area all my life (thirty-one years at this writing). I have caught a variety of fish there, including largemouth bass, crappie, northern pike, muskellunge, rock bass, and a variety of panfish. It's simply a nice place to visit and enjoy. I encourage everyone who hasn't seen it to visit and take a look around.

Some people don't share my enthusiasm about the TNT Area, however. The reports of the Mothman and the UFOs have taken their toll on many would-be visitors. I will be the first to admit that the TNT Area is a bit eerie at night. But, what can you expect from a huge Wildlife Management Area?

What sets this WMA apart from all others is the inclusion of the "igloos" scattered throughout. If you do come to visit, please be careful around the igloos and ponds. They are not places to be careless, and can be very dangerous.

If you can't find your way to the TNT Area, use the websites listed in our "Additional Resources" appendix (p. 163) for directions and information.

That having been said, enjoy the following history of the TNT Area.

During World War II, a lot of states were doing their part for the war efforts. In Mason County, West Virginia, a number of adjoining farms had been transformed into one such place.

Just six miles north of the small town of Point Pleasant, on State Route 62, an area was created to help war efforts by way of the manufacturing of *trinitrotoluene* (TNT). The new facility was officially named the West Virginia Ordnance Works.

Around one hundred above-ground bunkers, or "igloos," were built in order to store the TNT and other wartime products. The igloos were constructed of steel-reinforced concrete with ventilation shafts atop them. Each igloo was covered with dirt, which in turn was sewn with grass seed. The grass blended perfectly with the surrounding landscape, hiding the igloos from any air surveillance by enemy spies. All of the igloos were built with massive steel doors capable of withstanding tremendous blasts by enemy bombs.

One of the infamous "igloos." (Photo by Daniel Carter)

Below is an Environmental Protection Agency (EPA) description of the area:

> *The West Virginia Ordnance National Priority List (NPL) site is located near Point Pleasant, West Virginia. It is an 8,320-acre site used by the Army from 1942 to 1945 to produce TNT (trinitrotoluene). Soils around the operation's industrial area, process facilities, and industrial wastewater disposal system were contaminated with the TNT explosive, its by-products, and asbestos. When the site was decontaminated and decommissioned in 1945, the Army deeded the industrial portion to West Virginia, stipulating that it be used for wildlife management. The State created the McClintic State Wildlife Management Area on 2,785 acres, and the area is now used for recreational purposes. Other non-industrial portions of the original parcel are owned by the county or by private citizens. In 1981, Red Water seepage (liquid waste*

produced during the TNT manufacturing process) was observed near Pond 13 on the wildlife station. EPA and State investigations revealed that the groundwater and surface water were contaminated with explosive nitroaromatics. Buried lines associated with TNT manufacturing contained some crystalline TNT.

After World War II, sections of what is now called the "TNT Area" were sold or leased to a handful of different companies, including the study of biochemistry.

Many tests have been run on the area, searching for contaminants in the area's soil and water. The report released by the EPA is listed below:

Groundwater, seepage, soils, and the surface water on-site are contaminated with explosive nitroaromatic compounds including TNT, trinitrobenzene, and dinitrotoluene from former site operations as well as metals, including arsenic, lead and beryllium. Visitors to the wildlife management area may be exposed to contaminants by direct contact with or accidental ingestion of contaminated surface water or soils. The shallow groundwater has been shown to be contaminated and is moving toward nearby private residences with wells. No nitroaromatics have been detected in any of the 13 local water supply wells, but sewer lines, pits, and open manholes may contain reactive wastes, which may pose a safety and chemical hazard to people entering the site.

After finding the above, the EPA went to work cleaning up the area, making it a safe place for public recreation. The cleanup process released by the EPA is listed below:

The Remedial Actions (RAs) are being implemented by the Army Corp of Engineers as the lead agency for this site. The remedies selected to address the source of contamination are: (1) in-place flaming of reactive TNT residue on soil surfaces and installation of a 2-foot soil cover over highly contaminated areas; (2) disposal of asbestos off-site; and (3) excavation of reactive sewer lines, flashing of explosives, and backfilling of trenches from which lines are removed. These site cleanup activities are now complete. After completing these cleanup activities, the Army conducted an investigation and determined that damages occurred to natural resources (wetlands) during cleanup. As a result, replacement wetlands are now being constructed on a portion of the Site.

In 1991, cleanup activities began at the Red Water and Yellow Water Reservoir. Remedies include relocating Ponds 1 and 2, filling and capping the original Ponds 1 and 2, and extracting and treating the groundwater. The groundwater pump and treat system is installed and the final inspection was completed February of 1997.

The remedies originally selected to treat the Pond 13 wet well contamination has been determined to be technically impracticable. Subsequent investigations have determined that the contamination in this area is localized in discrete areas and remediation is being planned as a removal action.

A ROD for OU-11(Sellite Manufacturing Area) was completed during FY 2000. The risk assessment for OU-11 determined the risk to be within the acceptable EPA risk range which will result in a “No Action” ROD. Risk assessments for all currently identified OUs have been submitted for review. Also, all site investigation reports have been submitted for review. Additionally, the Point Pleasant Landfill has been identified as an area of concern by EPA, and is being considered for further investigation. At the time of this writing, the EPA is working with the lead agency and the WVDEP to develop proposed plans and RODs for OU-10 (South Acids Area, Toluene Storage Area, and the Cooling Tower Area) and OU-12 (North and South Powerhouses).

Additional actions that have been completed at the site include: removal of drums, soil, and debris from the "Toxic Swamp" area completed in 1994; removal of asbestos from the North and South Power Houses, Power Houses demolished and open pits and manholes filled completed in January of 1995; and removal of 32 drums from the OU-11 Sellite Manufacturing Area in 1999. Recently, "Decision Documents" were completed which indicated no further investigation or remedial actions will be necessary at four sites. The Site names are Tract 21 Area, Refueling Depot, Sewage Treatment Plant Outfall, and the Washout Area.[1]

— *Donnie Sergent, Jr.*

---

1. Source: Further information concerning this area and the EPA can be found by going to the website of the United States Environmental Protection Agency: http://www.epa.gov

The detailed Administrative Record can be examined at the following location: Mason County Public Library, Sixth and Viand Streets, Point Pleasant, WV 25550.

PART II
EYEWITNESS ACCOUNTS

One of the original eyewitnesses made this sketch of the Mothman. (Courtesy Linda Scarberry)

Chapter 3: The Interview

This book is to be used as a reference guide to facts about the Mothman, mainly to satisfy the questions thousands of people have already asked me via the Internet. In no way do we intend to prove the Mothman to either be real or a myth. This is up to you to decide after being presented with the known facts.

I have gathered information from many sources to compile the most in-depth collection to-date of materials about the Mothman. The most interesting of all these are the actual newspaper clippings and my interview with Linda Scarberry. Linda offered us authentic newspaper clippings to use in this documentary, which she had cut out and compiled dating back to 1966. This collection is like nothing I have ever seen. To be able to see the actual clippings was intriguing. Now, you can read them, too.

I went to high school with Linda's daughter, Dani, and spoke with her about the Mothman incidents as well. Dani wasn't old enough to remember much of what went on back then, as she was very young. After I concluded the interview, Dani was amazed at the information her mother had disclosed to me.

"She has never told anyone some of this stuff," Dani told me. "Some of it, I didn't even know. She must really trust you."

The First Sighting

It was November, 1966. The town of Point Pleasant, West Virginia was about to be shaken by a series of events like nothing else on the face of the earth. Linda Scarberry was one of the first people at the scene of the first Mothman sighting in the area. Below is the transcribed interview I did with Linda on July 11, 2001.

Take a journey back to that horror-filled night as Linda brings the past to the present in her first full-length, publicly-released interview—her complete account of the Mothman. Follow along directly from the source. Let your eyes and ears be deceived by "hear-say" no longer. Finally, the entire, true story is available. This is a piece of history and accumulation of events that scientists, reporters, authors, and many officials have been trying to uncover for decades. It is now at your fingertips.

Linda relayed her intent to me of getting the true story out in the open, once and for all, to clear up any "stories" that were floating around about what she saw, and has seen since. This was a huge concern of hers.

"If there's going to be a movie about it," Linda said, "I want everyone to know what really happened."

I would like to take this space in the book to say "Thank You" to Linda for her trust and honesty, and to let the world know how kind and sincere this woman truly is. What follows is an unrivaled account of what happened back during the early years of the Mothman sightings, and some very eerie accounts of what has happened since. I have transcribed the interview with Linda and she has proofread it. What follows is that interview.

For the purpose of privacy, Linda's current last name has been withheld.

Donnie Sergent, Jr.: For the record, please state your full name now and what your married name was back in 1966.

Linda: I would rather keep my current name private. My married name in 1966 was Linda Scarberry.

DS: First of all, thank you very much Linda for offering to do this exclusive interview with me. National investigators and journalists have tried to get this exclusive full-length interview and, understandably, you have declined in the past years for fear that your words would be twisted or changed. I understand that you've trusted only a couple of people with this information in the past, but have never given an extensive, detailed interview to anyone. Thank you for keeping this information honest, and thank you for your trust.

Linda: You're welcome. Thank you for doing the interview.

DS: First, let's clear something up for everyone. There is a lot of speculation about the use of drugs and alcohol when this creature was sighted. Were you using drugs or alcohol when you first sighted the Mothman in the TNT area?

Linda: Absolutely not. No one in the car at the time of the sighting was drinking or using drugs of any kind.

DS: A lot of national paranormal investigators, as well as other people, are curious to know what the atmosphere was like on that eerie night in the TNT area. Would you describe the time, date, and the general weather on the evening when you first sighted the Mothman?

Linda: It was cold and around 11:30 p.m., November 15, 1966. Both couples in the car that night were married. We [Linda, her ex-husband, and their two friends] were just out chasing parkers. It wasn't raining, or foggy, at all. It was a very clear, cold night.

DS: This creature has been described by many people. There have been many different reports of what the Mothman looks like. Would you describe, in detail, what it looked like? Its head, body, wings, etc. . .

Linda: It was about seven feet tall. It had wings that were visible on its back, the tips of the wings could be seen above its shoulders. The body of it was like a slender, muscular man, and was flesh-colored. It's wings were an ashen white in color. The wings looked like angel wings. Its face couldn't be seen, because the eyes simply hypnotized you when you looked into them. You didn't have to look directly into them. If you looked close to its face, your eyes were just drawn to its eyes. It wasn't that it didn't have a head, it was just that when your eyes got close to its head and neck area, the eyes consumed your vision, and you couldn't see anything but them. It had arms and legs, like a muscular man. When we first saw it, we had just topped a hill in the TNT area, and when the headlights of our car hit it, it looked directly at us, as if it was scared. It had one of its wings caught in a guide wire near a section of road close to the power plant, and was pulling on its wing with its hands, trying to free itself. Its hands were really big. It was really scared. We stopped the car and sat still while it was trying to free itself from the wire. We didn't sit there long, just long enough to scare it, I think. It seemed to think we were going to hurt it. We were all screaming, "Go! Go! Go!" But, we couldn't perform the actual action of leaving the scene. It was like we were hypnotized. It finally got its wing loose from the wire and ran into the power plant. I felt sorry for it. We talked about it with Mr. Keel and Mr. Drasin. We thought it might have been some sort of machine or something, possibly being controlled by the UFOs or whatever was in them. But, it was too much like an animal for that. Its movements were too smooth. It wasn't a machine.

DS: Did it make any distinctive sounds?

Linda: It didn't make any sounds, at all, when we saw it that time.

DS: After the shock of the initial sighting, were you more afraid of the creature's presence in the area or more inclined to find out more about it?

Linda: At first we were afraid of it. After it was out of sight, we wanted to know more about it. But, we didn't want to get very close to it, because we weren't sure whether or not it would try to hurt us. It had many opportunities that night to kill us, if it had wanted to. It seemed to me that it was more scared than anything.

DS: How long after you initially sighted the creature did you go to the police? And, what was their initial reaction to your report?

Linda: We went to the police about a half-hour after we initially sighted it. They didn't believe us, at first. They thought we were crazy, or on drugs. A lot of other people did, too. But, after they saw how scared we were, and found out that we weren't drinking, or on drugs, they started to believe us. We wouldn't have went to the police, but it kept following us. We saw it sitting in different places as we drove back down Route 62 toward Point Pleasant, and saw it sitting in various places once we got in town, too. It was as if it was letting us know that it could catch up to us, no matter where we went, or how fast we went there. When we first left the TNT area, it was sitting on the sign when we went around the bend and when the headlights hit it, it went straight up into the air, very fast. That's when it followed us and hit the top of the car two or three times while we were going over one hundred miles per hour down Route 62, toward Point Pleasant. The last place we saw it was sitting on top of the flood wall. It was sitting crouched down, with its arms around its legs and its wings tucked against its back. It didn't seem scared, then. I guess it figured out that we weren't going to hurt it, so it followed us. We didn't know what else to do but go to the police station.

DS: Did you have any strange or unusual feelings or reactions during the sighting?

Linda: We were all scared. It was like the creature was trying to communicate with us. We didn't know what was going on. We kept asking each other if we saw the same thing. We were confused and scared. We didn't have any odd feelings at all that night except being very scared. We didn't know what to do, where it came from, or what it was going to do.

DS: Have you seen the Mothman since the initial sighting?

Linda: Yes. I saw it after that on several occasions.

DS: What sticks out in your mind as the most memorable detail about any of the sightings?

Linda: Two occasions stick out in my mind, very vividly. The first is when it was trying to free itself on the first night I saw it in the TNT area by pulling on its wing with its hands. The second was about a month after we first saw it, when we lived on 13th Street. The roof slanted down at an angle from the upstairs bedroom window. I looked out that window one night and it was sitting on the roof, close to the window. It was sitting down with its arms around its legs and wings folded around itself, like it was trying to keep warm. It had its head turned sideways, looking in through the window, as if it was curious. By then, I had figured out that it didn't want to hurt me. I could just tell by the way it looked at me. I was very curious and wanted to try to communicate with it, but I still didn't know what it was, or where it came from, and was a little scared of it, still. It looked so lonely, but not scared anymore. It looked cold, too. It was really cold out that night.

DS: Where do you believe it came from, or how did it originate?

Linda: I'm still not sure. The only thing I can think of is it was sent here to distract us from other things going on at the time. Maybe from another planet. Maybe from another country. I'm not sure. There was more going on at this time than just the Mothman sightings. There were UFO reports. And, more importantly, Men In Black (MIB) reports that were far less reported than either of the other two. People were afraid of reporting the MIB. I don't know that I believe in flying saucers, but I have seen UFOs on many occasions. That doesn't make them flying saucers, but no one ever explained what all of them were to any of us in the town.

DS: Do you believe UFOs were in any way involved with the Mothman?

Linda: Oh yeah. They were so pretty. I saw one that looked like a blooming rose. It was all different colors, like the petals were coming out of it in all directions. And, the colors weren't anything like we would have, they were much brighter, simply beautiful.

DS: There were reports of Satanic rituals being performed in the TNT area, years ago. Do you believe Satanic rituals in the TNT area were in any way involved with the Mothman?

Linda: No. Not at all. We saw those people up there a couple of times. They always scattered when we came back by for the second time. They had a cross up on a tree out there one night when we drove by. When we drove back by, it was gone and so were they.

DS: Do you believe the U.S. Government was involved in a coverup concerning UFOs and the Mothman in the Point Pleasant area?

Linda: Oh yeah. I think so.

DS: Without revealing their names, how many people do you know personally who have seen the Mothman? And, have they seen it on more than one occasion?

Linda: Thirty to forty people. And, yes, they have.

DS: Do you believe there is more than one of these creatures?

Linda: I didn't until about a month and a half after we first sighted it. There were two power plants, the North Power Plant and the South Power Plant, one on each side of the main road. We were up there with John Keel and some other people. Mary Hyre saw the Mothman on the other side of one of the cars parked there at the same time a girl from Mason, West Virginia saw it while inside the power plant with John Keel. Mr. Keel, however, did not see the creature. So, we thought there may be two of them. But, after we talked about it, we couldn't put the time lines together exactly right, so it may have moved from one place to the other very fast. We could never be sure. Both people who saw it described the exact same thing.

DS: Do you feel that the creature has/had good or evil intentions?

Linda: I don't think it ever had evil intentions. It had numerous chances to harm, or even kill me and some other people, but it didn't. I know one woman who saw it, and she said it chased her and her family into their house. But, I think they were just scared, like we were when we first saw it, and thought it would try to hurt them. I think its main intention was to not get hurt itself. A lot of people tried to kill it, or capture it. I don't think it would have hurt anybody or anything. There was a rash of dog and animal killings and a lot of dogs that started turning up missing. A lot of people blamed that on the Mothman, but I don't think it was him. I think it was a person around the area doing all that.

DS: What do you believe the creature's purpose was or is?

Linda: To distract everyone from the MIB and the UFOs that were in the area at the time.

DS: Do you believe the Mothman was in any way linked to the collapse of the Silver Bridge? For example, do you believe the creature caused it to fall, or did it try to warn people about the upcoming tragedy?

Linda: I don't think it caused it to fall or had anything to do with it. If people saw it when the bridge fell, I would say the MIB had something to do with it drawing everyone's attention away from whatever they were doing. I do think the MIB had something to do with the collapse of the Silver Bridge. I was down on the river bank after the bridge fell. There were policemen everywhere, National Guard, emergency squads, cranes, all kinds of that type of stuff. I didn't see it, but I was told later that someone saw a few of the MIB standing around after the bridge fell.

DS: I received an e-mail from the last tractor-trailer driver across the bridge before it fell. He told me that he saw the Mothman fly around the front of his truck and looked for it in the sky, but it was gone, fast. Did you ever see the Mothman around the Silver Bridge area?

Linda: No. I believe it would have made sense, though. The Mothman would have been used to divert peoples' attention away from something the MIB were doing close by. There could have been something there the MIB didn't want that truck driver to see.

DS: Do you believe the Mothman was in any way linked to the curse of Chief Cornstalk?

Linda: Go down through this town and you'll think everything's linked to that. I don't think it had anything to do with the Mothman, but I believe the curse had an effect on the town. Businesses started closing up left and right, all at once.

DS: Do you believe the igloos in the TNT area could have been used as nesting or hiding spots for the Mothman?

Linda: I think it's possible, but I doubt it. I think it stayed in the caves behind the TNT area. John

Keel thought so, too. I know a lady that lived there at the time, and she saw it in that area several times. She agreed that it was probably spending most of its time in the caves in that area. The Mothman chased her daughter into their house. She thought it was trying to hurt the child, but again, I disagreed with her. It scared them pretty bad, but it was probably just trying to communicate with them.

DS: How have the Mothman sightings affected your personal life?

Linda: None of us have ever been the same after the first sighting. I still look over my shoulder. I feel like there's something behind me, or in the room with me. I still dream about it after thirty-five years. It's just something people will never be able to forget. It's really hard to talk about it, because a lot of people don't believe it. I've come to the point to where I really don't care if anyone believes me or not. If this thing is going to be made into a movie, I want the truth to be available for people to read or hear. The only people who haven't made fun of us is you, John Keel, Mary Hyre, and Dan Drasin. All the other reporters and news crews have made us out to be a bunch of kids that were drunk or on drugs up there that night. The police know that's not true, and so do we. So, what the others print and say is no concern of mine. I won't mention any names, but several people think the MIB had a hand in Mary Hyre's death. She died of a heart attack, but some think it was more than that. Mary knew a lot about the UFO situation and reports, as well as the MIB.

DS: How did you get in touch with John Keel? And, did he believe your story?

Linda: He got in touch with us. He and Dan Drasin contacted us about the sightings. John Keel believed us, because he'd taken similar reports of the UFO and Mothman sightings before contacting us. He believed every word of what we said. He never saw the Mothman. He never got to see it before he left the area. However, he did see the UFOs in the area.

DS: Why do you believe all the other reports, including those such as birds like wild cranes and large owls, are not what you have seen? What is different about the creature you saw compared to all the so-called "scientifically explainable" reports that have been made?

Linda: They looked nothing like what we saw. Someone killed a huge, white owl in the area and reporters flocked to the scene to report that the Mothman had been captured, at last. I felt like just sitting down and crying. You could tell by looking at the owl that it wasn't what was being reported. It wasn't nearly as big, and it was a bird. What we saw was no bird, much less an owl or a crane. Its body wasn't even close to either of those. I could see the muscles in the arms and legs of the Mothman. They were human-like. Not even close to a bird of any kind.

DS: What would you say to someone who says the creature never existed?

Linda: I would say they could believe what they wanted to believe. It doesn't matter to me anymore if someone believes me or not. I just want people who do know that this was more than a bird to have the facts before it all gets blown out of proportion again.

DS: If someone sees this creature, would you rather have them report the sighting to the authorities, or just keep it to themselves, enabling the creature to remain in seclusion?

Linda: I'd rather people keep it to themselves if they see it. It will just draw attention to wherever it is at the moment, and possibly get it killed. It had every chance in the world to harm us, and it didn't. I think if it was left alone it wouldn't bother anyone, now. I don't think it wants anything now, it just doesn't have anywhere where it belongs.

It was used for a diversion tactic when all the UFOs and MIB were around, and it was just left after it was all over. I think it's lonesome. But, people are afraid of it, and will try to kill it if its location is disclosed, so I'd rather everyone keep the sightings to themselves. I know if I ever see it again, I won't say a word.

DS: As of this very moment, Wednesday, July 11, 2001, do you think the creature is still in the Point Pleasant area?

Linda: No. I think it's still around, but not around this area.

DS: Do you believe this creature will ever be captured, or photographed?

Linda: No. I think it's too smart and fast to be captured. It may be photographed someday, but I doubt it. I don't think anyone is going to try to capture it. I think they'll try to kill it.

DS: Why do you think the mystery of the Mothman still intrigues people after thirty-five years?

Linda: I don't know for sure. Probably because it's so unusual.

DS: Concerning this last question, I will completely respect and accept your answer, no matter what it may be. Is there anything about your experiences with this creature that you will never share with anyone, including me?

Linda: Yes.

DS: Feel free to make any final statement about anything we haven't covered concerning this creature or UFOs in the Point Pleasant area that you feel people will find interesting or useful.

Linda: The whole situation in Point Pleasant was centered around the Mothman, but that wasn't the center of the problems here. The Mothman was simply a diversion. It was used as a way to draw peoples' attention away from what was really going on. It served its purpose, then after a while it wasn't seen anymore. It was mainly used for taking our attention away from what the MIB were doing. It was mainly sighted for about a year. The sightings slowed after the Silver Bridge fell.

The MIB wore black suits, black hats, and sunglasses. They drove black cars—Cadillacs, I think. I'm not sure about the make and models of the cars. One of the cars would follow us around. There were three men in the car. The police were all involved with the Mothman. Their attention wasn't on the MIB. At least, that's how it seemed. I don't know if anyone even mentioned the MIB to the police. Everyone was so afraid of them. Mr. Keel seemed to think that the Mothman was here to distract us from these men. I don't know if they came from outer space or not. They may have come from another country, we were never sure. We talked about that a lot. One of the journalists that accompanied Mr. Keel seemed to think so, too. They looked like human beings, but their skin was somewhat transparent. You could see the veins in their hands very clearly. Their fingers were longer than a normal person's fingers, as well. Daddy shook hands with them, and he said they were awkward in shaking hands. They seemed to not know what to do, or how to shake hands. Our next door neighbor shook hands with them, and he said the same thing.

We had to keep a crucifix above Dani's [Linda's oldest daughter] bed. From what I understand, the MIB were here for her until she was six years old. Me and four other girls all got pregnant at the same time. And, before you ask, no, it wasn't aliens or anything that got us pregnant. We've been asked that before. Mr. Keel thought that these MIB were here after the babies because they were especially intelligent. Dani is, in fact, exceptionally intelligent, and the other babies turned out to be, as well. The MIB could shape the children's minds up until they were six years old. They could make them believe what they wanted them to. After they turned six years old, their minds were already shaped by their parents and their general surroundings.

For some reason, the MIB were afraid of a crucifix. One of the men came into my bedroom one night. Me, my aunt, and Dani were all sleeping in the same bedroom. My aunt had a dream that was exactly what happened in the room while she was asleep. Dani was in the baby bed, right beside my bed. We had a crucifix at the foot of Dani's baby bed. Mr. Keel said there had to be gold on the crucifix, so that's what we got. At about midnight that night a man walked into the room. We had the kitchen light on because the baby was in the room, so we could easily get to her quickly if we needed to. The kitchen was right off the bedroom, so the light flooded into the bedroom a little. The man had coal-black hair, and wore a black and white checkered shirt and black pants. He had a crewcut haircut that was about an inch long, sticking straight up. He had dark eyes. He didn't look like the men in the suits. His skin wasn't as transparent as theirs was. The light was dim coming from the kitchen, but I could see him well enough. He just stood there and stared at me, never blinking his eyes once. After a few minutes, he took a cigarette out of his shirt pocket and lit it. When he did that, the gold crucifix reflected the light and caught his eye. He turned to look at it, as I did. When I turned back, he was gone. No sounds at all. I walked into the kitchen and sat down for a little while. When my aunt woke up, she came into the kitchen and said she just had a wild dream. She described exactly what happened in the room a few minutes before. It was very scary. I think they were there to take Dani that night. And, that if it wasn't for that crucifix shining when he lit his cigarette, they may have gotten her.

DS: How old was Dani at the time?

Linda: About five months old. I could tell by the look in his eyes he was there for a purpose. I couldn't move a muscle. I was numb.

DS: He didn't speak at all?

Linda: He never said a word. He just stood there, staring at me.

DS: Did he look at Dani in the baby bed?

Linda: No. He looked at me, then the crucifix, then was gone. All of us girls kept crucifixes about the babies' beds, or close to them. The MIB tried to kidnap one of the other girls' babies in New Haven, West Virginia. She saw the Mothman at the Mason golf course. She saw it in daylight. It followed her car down the road. That was around 3:00 p.m. in the afternoon. She was driving about sixty MPH. She said it stayed right beside the car for awhile then disappeared. She said it looked like it wasn't even trying to keep up with her, like it was easy for it to be going that fast. She believed the MIB was trying to take her little boy. She won't talk about it much. She's a relative of one of the people originally involved with the sighting reports.

Mary Hyre was one of the people who knew the most about everything that was going on at the time. Mr. Keel said she knew too much. It just completely took over her life.

DS: Mary Hyre worked for the Athens Messenger*?*

Linda: Yes. She worked down on Sixth Street in Point Pleasant. She would report her news to the *Athens Messenger*. She passed away at a young age. There was talk that the MIB had something to do with her death. Mr. Keel said that she had either received or made a phone call just before she died, I can't remember which. He said that it may have been involved with her death. She had either made a call to report something she knew, or had received a threatening call for her to stop reporting about the MIB. It was a tense time for a lot of people around here.

DS: What about your father? What was his take on all this?

Linda: My dad didn't believe anything like this. He didn't believe in superstitions and didn't believe in things like the Mothman. He said that if he hadn't seen the look on our faces when after we first sighted the Mothman, he wouldn't have believed us. He said the fact that we gave up our home to move in with him for safety also made him believe us. We were renting a home near Tiny's Drive-In in Point Pleasant at the time.

The day before we saw the Mothman, it was at our home, but I didn't know what it was. My husband was at work. It was about 11 p.m. at night. This awful noise above our home started and it scared me. It sounded like the flapping of wings all around the home. I was petrified. I was scared to death. It circled the home and kept hitting the roof for about fifteen to twenty minutes. I didn't know what was going on, or what was hitting the roof. I never did go outside. It stopped a few minutes before my husband got home. But, I still wouldn't go outside. He came home and didn't see or hear anything. The next night, while we were at TNT, we found out what it was.

We used to go to TNT all the time and drag race. People would meet us up there from Pomeroy, Ohio and Parkersburg, West Virginia, among other places. There were a lot of cars up there at any given time. People brought their kids and everything. It was really fun. It was the thing to do at the time. That's how we had fun back then. A lot of couples used to meet up there and camp out. We all had hot rod cars. That was our meeting place back then. That was the place to hang out. After the Mothman was sighted, no one wanted to go back out there, especially after dark. But, really, we shouldn't have felt that way, because we saw it in town, and other places too. But, we were afraid to go up there after dark after that.

DS: Did anyone from the government ever contact you?

Linda: No. They contacted Mr. Keel. They told

Mr. Keel that there wasn't enough evidence to investigate it. I think they investigated it, but kept it quiet. They just wanted people to keep believing that everyone was making the whole thing up. But, there were a little too many people seeing that stuff to be making it up, and everyone knew it, including the government. They didn't want to add fuel to the fire. They wanted everything to quiet down, and all the attention to be taken away from the TNT area for some reason.

The UFOs were everywhere up there and in the general Point Pleasant area. We could go out on our back porch and use daddy's binoculars to see them a little clearer. They looked like brightly-colored flowers. Again, the colors were more vivid than any I've ever seen in my life, including after that day.

One of the MIB walked through my neighbor's garage and scared him very badly. My neighbor asked the man three or four times what he wanted, but the man didn't answer him. The way he described the man, he looked exactly like the man that was in my bedroom. He had on the same type shirt, pants, and had the same hair. I don't know if it was the same man or not, but it could have been.

The Mothman was smart and knew how close to get to people, as to not get hurt. A lot of people I know wanted to kill it. They just wanted it out of their lives. They didn't want anything to do with it, at all. The wanted it to go away, and tried to make it go.

Somehow it knew I didn't want to hurt it, and that I felt sorry for it. I wanted to talk to it and find out if I could help it, and it seemed to know that. It kept showing up to me. I kept wondering, 'Why me? Why is it just coming around me?' When I would see it, I would tell someone in my family about it and they'd say, 'You didn't see anything. Just stop talking about it.' After a while of hearing that, I started ignoring it and it went away. I felt bad about that. I was always curious about it because it never once tried to hurt me, and it could have several times. It had every opportunity to hurt or even kill me if it would have wanted to. But, I'll be honest with you, I was still afraid of it. There was too much that I didn't know about it to feel completely comfortable around it.

The MIB went so far as to follow us through the drive-thru of a restaurant. We were afraid to turn around, and just looked in the mirror at them. There were three of them. Mary Hyre told me that the MIB that were at her office would pick up common objects, like a pencil, or a stapler, and study it, as if they didn't know what it was. Mr. Keel said that was a strong indication that the MIB weren't from our government. He said it was likely that they were not from this planet.

Mr. Keel told us that people had been telling him they talked to him and it wasn't him. It was someone who looked like him. He said it was probably the MIB. He told us there would probably be someone coming around to talk to us, claiming to be him. He told us to ask him a question that only Mr. Keel would know. He told us not to be taken advantage of by this man. He told us to reference Mr. Drasin, and that they knew nothing about what Mr. Drasin, Mr. Keel, and myself had talked about confidentially. If he did come around, we never saw him. We knew Mr. Keel very well. He was a very nice man. My ex-husband and I were staying at my daddy's house at the time. We stayed in the basement and Mr. Keel stayed upstairs for a good while during his stay in the area. Mr. Drasin stayed with us, too. Mr. Keel originally stayed at the Blue Fountain Motel in Gallipolis, Ohio, right across the Ohio River from Point Pleasant. We told him that he was more than welcome to stay with us, and he accepted.

DS: Again, thank you Linda for offering to do this interview and for sharing the facts with millions of curious people. My best to you and yours.

Linda: Thank you.

Chapter 4: Eyewitness Reports

Linda Scarberry and two other eyewitnesses wrote the following reports just days after the original Mothman sightings in November, 1966. All are part of the collection of documents belonging to Linda that were used in production of this book.

These reports were never part of the official public record; they have never before been published. Many of the individuals involved with the sightings have become quite reluctant to share their experiences with the public and wish to be left alone.

Therefore, in order to respect their privacy, their names have been withheld and replaced with a description—for example, "Eyewitness #1." In order to assure consistency, whenever the same individual is mentioned in any of the reports, he or she is indicated with the same description.

Each scanned page of handwritten text has been transcribed on the opposite page for readibility.

— Transcriptions by Jeff Wamsley

Linda Scarberry

We were riding through the TNT Area on a side road by the old Power house building around 12:00 on Tuesday night Nov 15, 1966 when we came over this small rise in the road. All at once [redacted] yelled for us to look at that thing in the road. I looked up and saw it go around the corner at the Old Power House. It didn't run but wobbled like it couldn't keep its balance. Its wings were spread just a little. We sat there a few seconds then [redacted] took off. I kept yelling for him to hurry. We didn't even stop for the curves. We got out on Route 62 and was coming down the road and that thing was sitting on the second hill when you come into the 1st bad curves. As soon as our lights hit it, it was

Linda Scarberry

We were riding through the TNT
Area on a side road by the
old Power house building around
12:00 on Tuesday night Nov. 15th, 1966
when we came over this small
rise in the road. All at once
[Eyewitness #3] yelled for us to look
at that thing in the road. I
looked up and saw it go around
the corner at the old Power
House. It didn't run but wobbled
like it couldn't keep it's balance.
It's wings were spread just a
little. We sat there a few
seconds then [Eyewitness #2] took off.
I kept yelling for him to hurry.
We didn't even stop for the
curves. We got out on
Route 62 and was coming
down the road and that thing
was sitting on the second
hill when you come into
the 1st bad curves. As soon
as our lights hit it, it was. . .

gone. It ~~[illegible]~~ spread its wings a little & went straight up into the air. ~~We came on down the road~~ When we got to the Armory it was flying over our car. We were going between 100 and 105 M.P.H. down that straight stretch and that thing was just gliding back and forth over the back end of the car. As we got there in front of the lights by the Resort it dived at our car and went away. I could hear the wings flapping as if ~~[illegible]~~ to get more speed as it went up. We were all terrified and kept yelling for to go faster. As we came into that straight stretch by C.C. Lewis' the thing was over our car again then it disappeared as we came into the lights

. . . gone. It spread its wings
a little and went straight up into
the air.
When we got
to the armory it was flying
over our car. We were going
between 100 and 105 mph down
that straight stretch and that
thing was just gliding back
and forth over the back end
of the car. As we got there
in front of the lights by the
Resort it dived at our car
and went away. I could
hear the wings flapping as
if to get more speed as
it went up. We were all
terrified and kept yelling
for [Eyewitness #2] to go faster. As
we came into that straight
stretch by C. C. Lewis' [farm] the
thing was over our car
again. Then it disappeared
as we came into the lights. . .

3/

by C.C. Lewis' Gates. We went
on down town and stopped
at Dairy Land and tried to decide
what to do. We just sat there
& looked at each other. I
wanted to go to the police but
[redacted] & [redacted] kept saying they'd
just laugh at us We talked
about it awhile and
[redacted] & [redacted] wanted to go back
up the road [redacted] & I kept
trying to talk them out of it
and finally when we got to
C.C. Lewis' Gate they decided
they didn't want to go back
up so we turned around As
we were turning we saw
a big dead dog laying along the
road. When we were
almost turned around this
thing jumped out from behind
something and leaped over
our car and went through
the field on the other side

. . . by C.C. Lewis' gates. We went
on downtown and stopped
at Dairyland and tried to decide
what to do. We just sat there
and looked at each other. I
wanted to go to the police but
[Eyewitness #3] and [Eyewitness #2] kept saying they'd
just laugh at us. We talked
about it awhile and
[Eyewitness #2] and [Eyewitness #3] wanted to go back
up the road. [Eyewitness #1] and I kept
trying to talk them out of it
and finally when we got to
C.C. Lewis' gate they decided
they didn't want to go back
up so we turned around. As
we were turning we saw
a big dead dog laying along the
road. When we were
almost turned around this
thing jumped out from behind
something and leaped over
our car and went through
the field on the other side. . .

of the road. We decided to go to
the police then and went down
and around Tiny's Drive Inn
looking for them. [redacted]
was outside the Drive Inn getting
ready to take a couple loops
home so we told him about
seeing this thing and asked
him to call the police. After
the police came we went
back up the road in
our car with [redacted] &
the police about 1/2 mile behind
us & I saw it then in
a pasture field with its wings
out a little walking towards
the car then it went up in
the air & came at the car
A [redacted] car lights came over
the rise in the
road & the lights shined on
it – it disappeared. We went
up & down the road
looking for it but didn't see

. . . of the road. We decided to go to
the police then and went down
and around Tiny's Drive-In
looking for them. [Eyewitness #4]
was outside the Drive Inn getting
ready to take a couple boys
home so we told him about
seeing this thing and asked
him to call the police. After
the police came we went
back up the road in
our car with [Eyewitness #4] and
the police about 1/2 mile behind
us. I saw it then in
a pasture field with its wings
out a little walking towards
the car then it went up in
the air and came at the car.
As [Eyewitness #4]'s car lights came over
the rise in the
road and the lights shined on
it, it disappeared. We went
up and down the road
looking for it but didn't see. . .

3/

any more. We went back down
to the drive inn & got in
[redacted] car & went back up. We
finally found [redacted]
& got with him & went to
the Powerhouse building. We
sat there with our lights out
for about 15 or 20 minutes
when I heard that squeaking
sound like a mouse only a
lot stronger. A shadow went
across the building & the
dogs started barking over on
the hill across from us [redacted]
& I saw the red eyes
then & told [redacted]. He
shined the lights right on them
without being told where
they were. We saw dust
coming from the ground or
somewhere as [redacted] moved
the spot light around. We
finally left and came ~~home~~
~~[illegible]~~ to the trailer

. . . anymore. We went back down
to the drive in and got in
[Eyewitness #4]'s car and went back up. We
finally found [Eyewitness #5]
and got with him and went to
the powerhouse building. We
sat there with our lights out
for about 15 or 20 minutes
when I heard that squeaking
sound like a mouse only a
lot stronger. A shadow went
across the building and the
dogs started barking over on
the hill across from us. [Eyewitness #1]
and I saw the red eyes
then and told [Eyewitness #5]. He
shined the lights right on them
without being told where
they were. We saw dust
coming from the ground or
somewhere as [Eyewitness #5] moved
the spotlight around. We
finally left and came
to the trailer. . . .

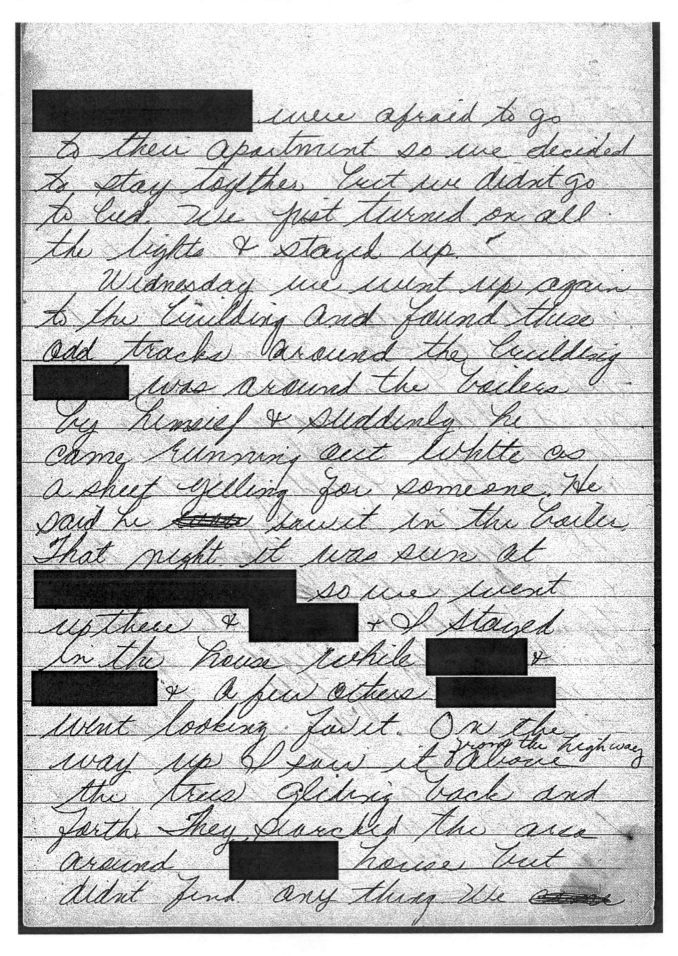

[redacted] were afraid to go to their apartment so we decided to stay together but we didn't go to bed. We just turned on all the lights & stayed up.

Wednesday we went up again to the building and found these odd tracks around the building [redacted] was around the boilers by himself & suddenly he came running out white as a sheet yelling for someone. He said he ~~[crossed out]~~ saw it in the boiler. That night it was seen at [redacted] so we went up there & [redacted] & I stayed in the house while [redacted] & [redacted] & a few others [redacted] went looking for it. On the way up I saw it from the highway above the trees gliding back and forth. They searched the area around [redacted] house but didn't find any thing. We ~~[crossed out]~~

[Two of them] were afraid to go
to their apartment so we decided
to stay together but we didn't go
to bed. We just turned on all
the lights and stayed up.
Wednesday we went up again
to the building and found these
odd tracks around the building.
[Eyewitness #3] was around the boilers
by himself and suddenly he
came running out white as
a sheet yelling for someone. He
said he saw it in the boiler.
That night it was seen at
[Eyewitness #6]'s so we went
up there and [Eyewitness #1] and I stayed
in the house while [Eyewitness #3] and
[Eyewitness #2] and a few others [bystanders]
went looking for it. On the
way up I saw it from the highway above
the trees gliding back and
forth. They searched the area
around [Eyewitness #6]'s house but
didn't find anything. We. . .

41

started home around 12:30 & I saw
it in one of the maintence
building. [redacted] & I started crying
& [redacted] took off & I kept thinking
about that thing following
us again but it didnt. We
went to my mothers and I
went all to pieces.
[redacted] & my Dad took me
down to the hospital. I finally
got back home & we
all stayed together that night again
but didnt go to bed till 3
or 4 o'clock. We were
still afraid to go to sleep.
The next day, Thurs we went
went back up with reporters
& we all heard a clanging
noise from inside the building.
[redacted], [redacted] & the reporters
went back in & found the
boiler door open that [redacted]
had shut when he left a few
minutes before that. That night

. . . started home around 12:30 and I saw
it in one of the maintenance
buildings. [Eyewitness #1] and I started crying
and [Eyewitness #2] took off. I kept thinking
about that thing following
us again but it didn't. We
went to my mothers' and I
went all to pieces.
[Eyewitness #2] and my dad took me
down to the hospital. I finally
got back home and we
all stayed together that night again
but didn't go to bed till 3
or 4 o'clock. We were
still afraid to go to sleep.
The next day Thursday we went
back up with reporters
and we all heard a clanging
noise from inside the building.
[Eyewitness #2] , [Eyewitness #3] and the reporters
went back in and found the
boiler door open that [Eyewitness #3]
had shut when he left a few
minutes before that. That night. . .

we went back up and Mary Hyre & I saw the eyes inside the fenced off place byside the Power house building on the way home I saw its eyes back in some trees from the road as the car went past & looked back & could see it form. That is the last time I have seen it. To me it just looks like a man with wings. It has a body shape form with wings on its back that come around it. It has muscular legs like a man and fiery-red eyes that glow when the lights hit it. There was no glow about it until the lights hit it. I couldn't see its head or arms. I don't know if the eyes are even in a head. When we came down the straight stretch by the Armory it didnt

It was a dingy grey color

. . . we went back up and Mary
Hyre and I saw the eyes inside the
fenced off place beside the
Power house building. On the
way home I saw its eyes
back in some trees from the road
as the car went past and looked
back and could see its form. That
is the last time I have
seen it. To me it just looks
like a man with wings. It
has a body shape form with
[It was a dirty grey color.]
wings on its back that come
around it. It has muscular
legs like a man and fiery-red
eyes that glow when the lights
hit it. There was no glowing
about it until the lights hit it.
I couldn't see its head or
arms. I don't know if the
eyes are even in a head.
When we came down the straight stretch
by the armory it didn't. . .

5/

even seem like it had any trouble keeping up with us. It must have had very powerful wings. At no time did this thing ~~fly~~ fly at us from the front of the car. It stayed over the back end of the car while it was chasing us. It seemed to be afraid of lights but I read in the paper today that it has been seen in the day time in town. That I don't understand. The prints we found at Lewis' gate, ~~the dog was~~ at Trash Powerhouses and at [redacted] They look like 2 horse shoes put together but they're smooth.

I know people are laughing at us but its no laughing matter. Will never forget this thing. It has affected our lifes in many ways. I am keeping going on nerve and

*. . . even seem like it had any trouble
keeping up with us. It must
have had very powerful wings.
At no time did this thing
fly at us from the front of
the car. It stayed over the
back end of the car while it
was chasing us. It seemed to
be afraid of lights but I
read in the paper today that
it has been seen in the
day time in town. That I
don't understand. The prints
we found at C. C. Lewis' gate
and at both
Powerhouses and at [Eyewitness #6]'s. . . .
They looked like 2 horse shoes
put together but they're smooth.*

*I know people are laughing
at us but it's no laughing
matter. We'll never forget this
thing. It has affected our
lives in many ways. I am
keeping going on nerve and. . .*

sleeping pills. When it gets dark I feel the fear creeping over me. ~~When~~ when I go any place & ~~the~~ I ~~out~~ automatically look up and out the windows. ~~I~~ I am afraid to sleep at night so I lay awake sometimes crying with fear. When I do sleep or go to bed I ~~d~~ the lights burn all night. Even in the daylight I'm ~~afra~~ afraid to be by myself. I walk around in my own house expecting to see that thing. I close my eyes day or night and I can see those red fiery eyes staring at me. Every little noise scares me to death. I can stand in a crowd & hear people talking about us & laughing. People have said we were probably "liquored up" but we were not. They go up there expecting to see it but then they say they dont believe ~~u~~ us. We have seen

. . . sleeping pills. When it gets dark
I feel the fear creeping over
me. When I go anyplace I
automatically look up and
out the windows. I am afraid
to sleep at night so I lay awake
sometimes crying with fear. When
I do sleep or go to bed the
lights burn all night. Even in
the daylight I'm afraid to
be by myself. I walk around
in my own house expecting to
see that thing. I close my eyes
day or night and I can see
those red fiery eyes staring
at me. Every little noise scares
me to death. I can stand in
a crowd and hear people talking
about us and laughing. People have
said we were probably "liquored
up" but we were NOT. They
go up there expecting to see it
but then they say they don't
believe us. We HAVE seen. . .

6/

it so we know what to look for and we're constantly looking not because we want to see it - but because we're afraid we'll see it again. Out of all the phone calls we've gotten not one minister has called to help us or try to explain what it is. We all agree we'd like to talk to a minister about it but no one takes us that serious. One minister even laughed & said they'd finally run the devil out of their church & that's what we saw. We've been harrassed & laughed at and called crazy. We can't just go up there & hand it to people on a silver platter like they seem to want us to do. We are never really going to get over our fear until we find out for sure what this

. . . it so we know what to look
for and we are constantly looking—
not because we want to
see it—but because we're
afraid we'll see it again. Out
of all the phone calls we've gotten
not one minister has called to
help us or try to explain what
it is. We all agree we'd like
to talk to a minister about it but
no one takes us that serious.
One minister even laughed and
said they'd finally run the
devil out of their church
and that's what we
saw. We've been harassed and
laughed at and called crazy.
We just can't go up there
and hand it to people on a
silver platter like they seem
to want us to do. We are
never really going to get over
our fear until we
find out for sure what this. . .

7/

thing is. I know I'll never forget
it I dont think anyone can
who has seen it.

. . . thing is. I know I'll never forget
it. I don't think anyone can
who has seen it.

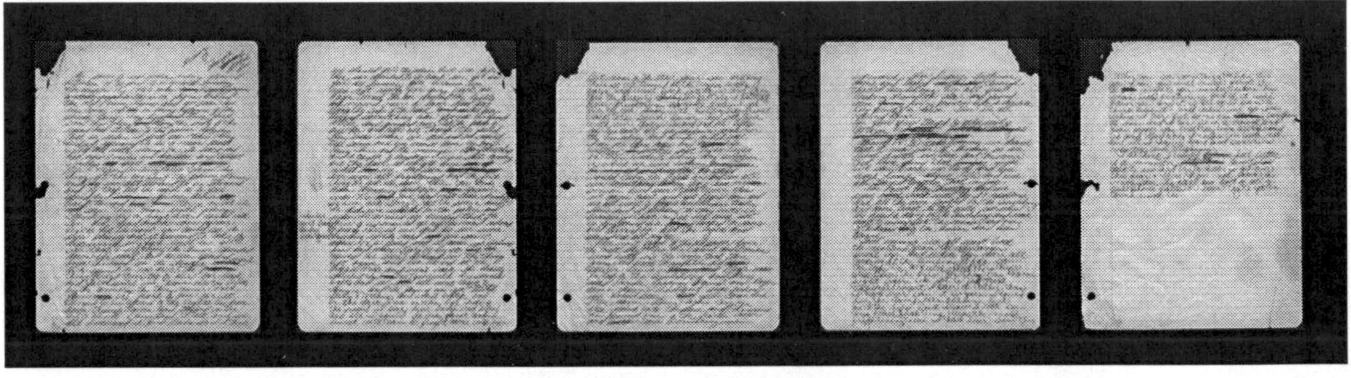

Eyewitness #1

The four of us were riding around between 11:30 and 12:00 o'clock Tuesday, November 15th, 1966, when we came in from behind the old powerhouse and as soon as we came up in seeing distance of the power house [Eyewitness #3] first seen this thing along the side of the road and it ran to the power house, that is when I first saw this thing which appeared to be a man about 6 feet tall with wings on its back and red eyes 2 inches in diameter and about 6 inches apart. [The other two] also saw this thing at the corner of the power house and we all seemed to be stunned and he took off out the road at a fast speed and as we drove back toward town on Rt. 62 we saw this man with wings standing on a bank but I could not see his head and as soon as our lights hit the bank you could see its eyes plainly and it seemed to take off upward very fast, well we all saw that, and [Eyewitness #2] the driver speeded down the road and as we speeded down the road on the straight stretch at a speed of 100 or 105 mph the thing glided over top of our car back and forth until we drove into the lights by the armory the thing never once flew in front of our car. It seemed to be afraid of the lights. We drove down through town and stopped in the lights at about Dairyland to talk and we all discussed it and Linda said, "I think we should go to the police," but we didn't. Then we decided to go back. We got as far as [C.C.] Lewis' gate because we were not really for going back. As [Eyewitness #2] turned the car around the lights moved over a large dead dog along the side of the road. As we turned something ran from behind a tree and jumped over top the back of our car and ran out through the field. Then was when we decided we should tell someone. We went down by Tiny's Drive-in and [Eyewitness #4] and a couple others were just coming out the door so we told him what we had seen. We were all frightened and the first thing he asked us was, "Have you kids been drinking?" and our answer was, "No, we had not been drinking." So we asked [Eyewitness #4] to call the police and he did. We waited on the police and when they arrived we decided that the four of us would go up the road ahead of everyone. So we all did. As we were driving up the road we saw it again in a field and it came up behind us and when [Eyewitness #4]'s lights could be seen behind us the thing left again and we turned at the traffic circle and went back. [Eyewitness #5] searched the tree tops with his search lights and we all went back to Tiny's and the four of us got in the car with [Eyewitness #4] and went back and in the dark area on the left side of the road I seen two large red eyes and all I could do was point and I burst into tears as fright came into me. But none of the other four saw anything there so we turned at the traffic circle again and went back into town and [Eyewitness #4] told [Eyewitness #5] of our frightening experience and we got into the car with [Eyewitness #5] and went back to the power house and sat there with our doors locked and our lights off. We could all see shadows coming over the building and I said I can see those eyes and [Eyewitness #5] put the spotlight right on them without asking any direction in which we were looking. [Eyewitness #5] turned the lights on and we all seen something looking like dust or smoke. We seen that twice then we came back and got [Eyewitness #2]'s car and we all went to the trailer. We decided to stay with them that night. We were all so frightened we locked the doors and turned on all the lights and stayed up all night. We went back to the old power house the next day and them and [Eyewitness #7] went with us. The men took their guns and went through the old power house. [Eyewitness #2] was on top of the building and [Eyewitness #3] was inside looking around and [Eyewitness #2] came down to the outside when we heard [Eyewitness #3] yell come back here. [Eyewitness #3] came down before anyone else went into the place and he said he opened one of the boiler doors and saw something move upward. Then [Eyewitness #8] came and looked through the old building. We all were looking around the place and found some funny prints like a double hoof print of a horse. Then we all returned home. We stayed together most of the time. About 9:30 that evening we heard that it was seen at [Eyewitness #6]'s so we went directly up there and the men took their guns that night. We saw tracks up there and we went home about 12:30 and we all stayed together that night. The next day was Thursday and we went back with the T.V. reporters and all the men looked in the building and came back to talk with us when they heard a clang in the building and went back to investigate the noise and one of the doors of the boilers had been opened. That evening we all went back. The reporters from the messenger went up. While they were all looking at the building Linda saw the eyes in a field and Mrs. Hyre also saw the eyes. On the way home right before we got to the Point Pleasant resort I saw it better than I had ever saw it before. I could see the complete outline of it and the eyes but I could not any head. That time was the most frightening time I had ever saw this. When you see something like this you know you will never forget it. At night you wonder where this man-like creature is and if it will harm you and it is all I seem to think about. And when we go somewhere I can fell someone laughing at me. And I can be in a crowd and hear people say, "Well they were all liquored up," and God only knows we were not. But all I have heard and seen is news reporters and telephones. I do think I would feel better if a minister would come to talk to us and try to help us get over this fear. There has not been a minister to call us out of all our phone calls or even try to get in touch with us.

Eyewitness #2

Tuesday night about 12 o'clock while riding in the TNT Area we came upon this thing. It was in the shape of a man with wings. This thing stood about 6 feet tall with wings on its back. It was light grey in color, with red eyes about 2 inches in diameter 6 to 8 inches apart. When we came up over a rise in the road in front of the power house [Eyewitness #3] saw these large red eyes. He pointed the eyes out to me and when we all looked it was going around the corner of the building. This thing runs awkward with its wings out to its side. After we stopped and looked at each other I took off out the road toward the highway. When we came to the traffic circle and turned south on 62 we saw it again. It was on the bank on the left side of the road. This is where we could see it the best. But when the car lights shown on it, it moved its wings out to its side and went straight up in the air. We didn't see it again till we were on the straight road in front of the experiment farm when it came over the car again. I speeded up to 100 mph and it glided over the car till we came to the curve at the armory. Then it was gone. We came on in to town. This thing must have been afraid of lights because it wouldn't come in to town. We went downtown and stopped. We wanted to tell the police but we were going to go back up to see for sure that it was still up the road. But when we going up through town we decided we didn't want to go back up. So I turned around at the gate at the C. C. Lewis farm. When I turned around a dead dog was lying along the road. As I turned and started back down the road this thing came out from behind where the dog was and went over the back of the car and out through the field on the other side of the road.

Then we went down to Tiny's Drive-in and told [Eyewitness #4] what we saw and told him to call the police. When the police got there [Eyewitness #4] and the police followed us back up the road where we saw it again. The dog was gone. But when his car came over the hill behind us it was gone. From there we went back to this field but didn't see it again. So we went down to town. Then we went with the deputy sheriff back to the power plant and stopped. We sat in the car and saw dust or smoke coming up from the coal yard beside the plant. From there we went back and got in the car and went home.

Next day / Wednesday—The next day we went back to the power plant and looked around where [Eyewitness #3] saw it again in a boiler inside the plant. Then Wednesday night it was seen at [Eyewitness #6]'s home in the TNT Area. We went up to [Eyewitness #6]'s home the same night and found a footprint this thing had made.

Thursday—Thursday we went up to the plant with reporters and went through it. While we were inside [Eyewitness #3] shuts the boiler door. When we were outside we heard a loud noise. We went back inside and the door was open. What this thing looked like-it is about 6 feet tall with large wings on its back. It has a shape of a man. It has two red eyes about 2 inches in diameter 6 to 8 inches apart. A wing spread of 10 feet. This thing whatever it is is definitely not a crane or goose or balloon or any of the things it has been called. I have seen it and know what it looks like.

PART III

THE PUBLIC RECORD: Newspaper Clippings

These are authentic newspaper clippings collected by Linda Scarberry. She had saved them over the years to chronicle the events of the Mothman phenomenon and the happenings around Point Pleasant, West Virginia, and surrounding areas.

Many of the clippings are unidentifiable as to their original source. Exhaustive efforts were made to determine their origins; it is likely that the uncredited clippings came from one of the following sources:

- *The Athens Messenger*, Athens, Ohio;
- *The Point Pleasant Register*, Point Pleasant, West Virginia; or,
- *The Gallipolis Daily Tribune*, Gallipolis, Ohio.

All clippings are reprinted by permission.

(If any reader recognizes the source of an unidentified piece, please write the authors—in care of the publisher—in order to give proper credit in future printings.)

oint Pleasant Register

Mason County's Daily Newspaper

Point Pleasant, W. Va. WEDNESDAY, NOVEMBER 16, 1966 Price 5c

in Crash Kills 30, Injures Over 200

Couples See Man-Sized Bird...Creature...Something!

"It was a bird...or something. It definitely wasn't a flying saucer."

Two Point Pleasant couples said today they encountered a man-sized, bird-like creature in the TNT area about midnight last night.

Sheriff's deputies and City Police went to the scene about 2 o'clock this morning but were unable to spot anything.

But the two young men telling their story this morning were dead serious, and asserted they hadn't been drinking.

Steve Mallette of 3305 Jackson Avenue and Roger Scarberry of 609 30th Street described the thing as being about six or seven feet tall, having a wing span of 10 feet and red eyes about two inches in diameter and six inches apart.

"It was like a man with wings," Mallette said. "It wasn' like anything you'd see on TV or in a monster movie."

The men and their wives were in Scarberry's car between 11:30 p.m. and midnight when they spotted the creature near the old power plant adjacent to the old National Guard Armory buildings.

The creature was seen standing on three occasions and was described as being extremely fast ("it flew about 100 miles an hour") in flight but was a clumsey runner.

Deputy Millard Halstead said he had seen dust in the vicinity of a coal field. But "it could have been" caused by the bird, he said.

"I'm a hard guy to scare" Scarberry said, "but last night I was for getting out of there."

They did just that, but the "thing" followed them. They said it was hovering over the car, apparently gliding, until they reached the National Guard Armory on Route 62.

"We went downtown, turned around, and went back and there it was again," Mallette said. "It seemed to be waiting on us." He said the light-grey-like creature then scurried through a field. It also had flown across the top of the car.

"It apparently is afraid of light," Mallette reasoned, "and maybe it thought it was scaring us off."

The young men said they saw the creature's eyes, which glowed red, only when their lights shined on it. And it seemed to want to get away from the lights.

They said it looked like a "man with wings" but that its head was "not an outstanding characteristic."

SEE STORY NO 1 PAGE 3

The newspaper article that broke the story locally in Point Pleasant—not the lead story, but nonetheless very prominent.

oint Pleasant R

Mason County's Daily Newspaper

Point Pleasant, W. Va.

ain Crash Kills 30,

Couples See Man-Sized Bi

"It was a bird...or some-thing. It definitely wasn't a fly-ing saucer."

Two Point Pleasant couples said today they encountered a man-sized, bird-like creature in the TNT area about midnight last night.

Sheriff's deputies and City Police went to the scene about 2 o'clock this morning but were unable to spot anything.

But the two young men tell-ing their story this morning were dead serious, and assert-ed they hadn't been drinking.

Steve Mallette of 3305 Jackson Avenue and Roger Scarberry of 809 30th Street described the thing as being about six or sev-en feet tall, having a wing span of 10 feet and red eyes about two inches in diameter and six inches apart.

"It was like a man with wings," Mallette said. "It wasn' like anything you'd see on TV or in a monster movie.."

The men and their wives were in Scarberry's car be-tween 11:30 p.m. and midnight when they spotted the creature near the old power plant adja-cent to the old National Guard Armory buildings.

The creature was seen stand-ing on three occasions and was described as being extremely fast ("it flew about 100 miles

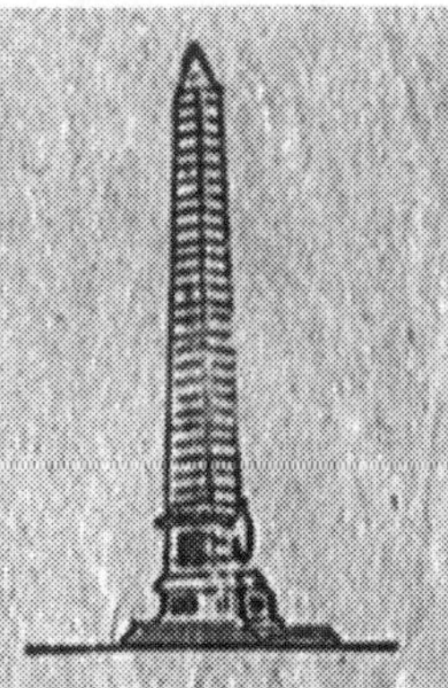

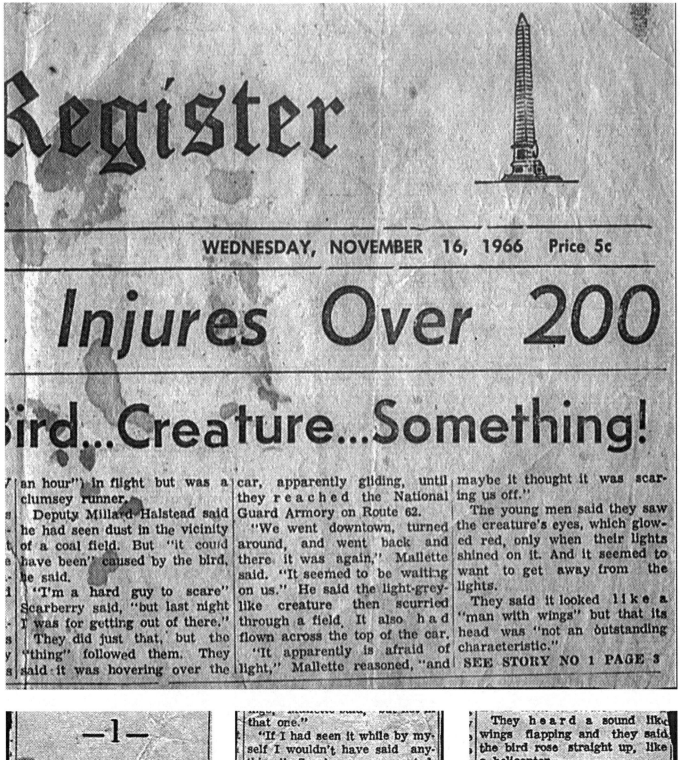

WEDNESDAY, NOVEMBER 16, 1966 Price 5c

Injures Over 200

Bird...Creature...Something!

an hour") in flight but was a clumsey runner.

Deputy Millard Halstead said he had seen dust in the vicinity of a coal field. But "it could have been" caused by the bird, he said.

"I'm a hard guy to scare" Scarberry said, "but last night I was for getting out of there."

They did just that, but the "thing" followed them. They said it was hovering over the car, apparently gliding, until they reached the National Guard Armory on Route 62.

"We went downtown, turned around, and went back and there it was again," Mallette said. "It seemed to be waiting on us." He said the light-grey-like creature then scurried through a field. It also had flown across the top of the car.

"It apparently is afraid of light," Mallette reasoned, "and maybe it thought it was scaring us off."

The young men said they saw the creature's eyes, which glowed red, only when their lights shined on it. And it seemed to want to get away from the lights.

They said it looked like a "man with wings" but that its head was "not an outstanding characteristic."

SEE STORY NO 1 PAGE 3

—1—

Both were slightly pale and tired from lack of sleep during the night following their harrowing experience.

They speculated that the thing was living in the vacant power plant, possibly in one of the huge boilers. "There are pigeons in all the other buildings," Mallette said, "but not in that one."

"If I had seen it while by myself I wouldn't have said anything," Scarberry commented, "but there were four of us who saw it."

They said it didn't resemble a bat in any way, but "maybe what you would visualize as an angel."

The last time they saw it was at the gate of the C. C. Lewis farm on Route 62.

They heard a sound like wings flapping and they said the bird rose straight up, like a helicopter.

"This doesn't have an explanation to it," Mallette said, "It was an animal but nothing like I've seen before."

Are they going back to look for the creature?

"Yes," Mallette said, "this afternoon and again tonight."

"Today," Scarberry said, "but tonight, I don't know!"

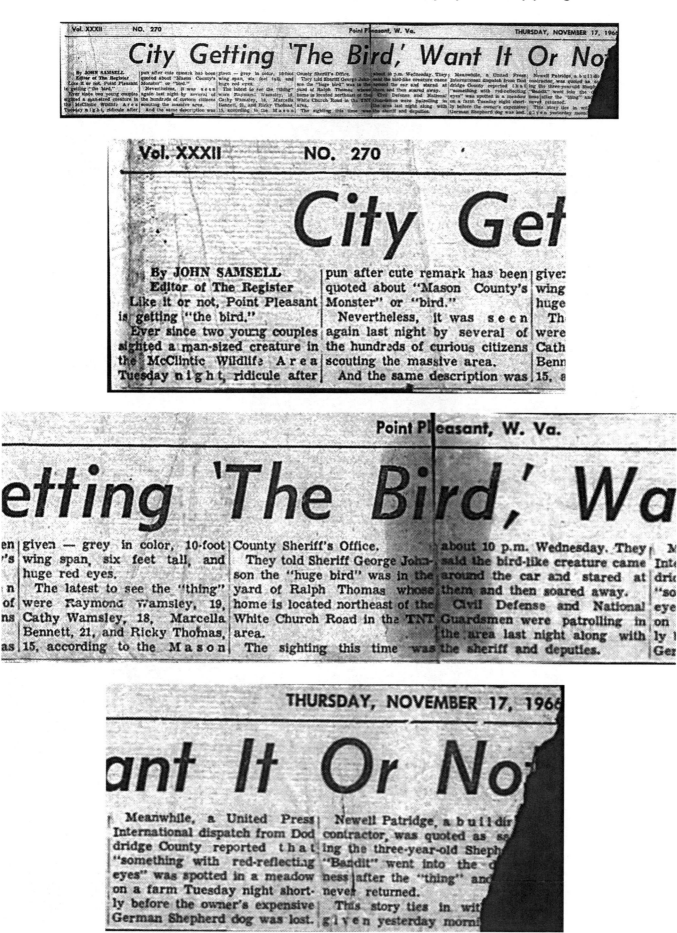

Vol. XXXII NO. 270 Point Pleasant, W. Va. THURSDAY, NOVEMBER 17, 196

City Getting 'The Bird,' Want It Or No

By JOHN SAMSELL
Editor of The Register

Like it or not, Point Pleasant is getting "the bird."

Ever since two young couples sighted a man-sized creature in the McClintic Wildlife Area Tuesday night, ridicule after pun after cute remark has been quoted about "Mason County's Monster" or "bird."

Nevertheless, it was seen again last night by several of the hundreds of curious citizens scouting the massive area.

And the same description was given — grey in color, 10-foot wing span, six feet tall, and huge red eyes.

The latest to see the "thing" were Raymond Wamsley, 19, Cathy Wamsley, 18, Marcella Bennett, 21, and Ricky Thomas, 15, according to the Mason County Sheriff's Office.

They told Sheriff George Johnson the "huge bird" was in the yard of Ralph Thomas whose home is located northeast of the White Church Road in the TNT area.

The sighting this time was about 10 p.m. Wednesday. They said the bird-like creature came around the car and stared at them and then soared away.

Civil Defense and National Guardsmen were patrolling in the area last night along with the sheriff and deputies.

Meanwhile, a United Press International dispatch from Doddridge County reported that "something with red-reflecting eyes" was spotted in a meadow on a farm Tuesday night shortly before the owner's expensive German Shepherd dog was lost.

Newell Patridge, a buildi contractor, was quoted as sa ing the three-year-old Sheph "Bandit" went into the d ness after the "thing" and never returned.

This story ties in wit given yesterday morni

-2-

was gone and the bird was standing near the C.C. Lewis farm gate.

The "thing," which has been described by clever writers and newscasters throughout the country as a "monster moth," "red-eyed demon" and "bird-man," was spotted near here about 90 minutes after the Doddridge County dog disappeared.

Patridge said his flashlight picked up "two red reflections" in his meadow and at this the dog's hair stood up, he bared his teeth and rushed into the woods.

Doddridge County is approximately 60 miles from here — as the "bird" flies. And the local couples said the creature they saw traveled about 100 miles an hour.

Officials at McClintic today wouldn't hazard a guess at what the bird might be. But many others would.

Sheriff Johnson said the youths had "seen something" unusual to scare them." He theorized it may have been an "oversized Shitepoke, possibly a freak of nature." (This bird is also known as a "Shagpoke" and actually is a large bird with spindly legs, long wing spread, web-feet and lives around water, and makes a "raucous noise," they say.)

The bird mentioned above is sometimes referred to as a green heron and it roosts in day and feeds at night.

Another theory is that a

day and feeds at night.

Another theory is that a

South American vulture which has been seen as far north as Canada. And, reportedly, its flight path (pre-arranged, of course) is through this area.

Other observers feel it might be a Canadian goose, since many have gathered at McClintic ponds on their way south.

Nevertheless, there is something out there, and the curiosity won't cease until it's found — if ever.

UPI Reporter Robert M. Gornall was here last evening to get the story and his dispatch is being carried to distant points. In it he told of seeing "oval-shaped footprints measuring about 4½ inches across and fresh animal droppings none of the natives in the party could identify."

He asked the question: Is there a "Mason County Monster?"

While the "bird" is the talk of the town at the moment, the incident also is bringing prominence to the city.

One citizen exclaimed: "After all, it's a bird sanctuary!" An Mayor D. B. Morgan was cited

as the "instigator" for having signed a proclamation recently for the sanctuary.

While cars jammed the TNT area last night, it was noticeable that the Audobon Society was missing the boat. No one was handing out membershi[p] applications.

Winged, Red-Eyed 'Thing' Chases Point Couples Across Countryside

By MARY HYRE
Point Pleasant Correspondent

POINT PLEASANT — What stands six feet tall, has wings, two big red eyes six inches apart and glides along behind an auto at 100 miles an hour?

Don't know? Well, neither do four Point Pleasant residents who were chased by a weird "man-like thing" Tuesday night.

Two young Mason County married couples today told of being chased by the "strange creature" around midnight Tuesday.

Mr. and Mrs. Steve Mallette, 3505 Jackson Ave., and Mr. and Mrs. Roger Scarberry, 809½ 30th St., described their hair-raising experiences, which began in the TNT area.

The two couples were riding in a car and as the auto crested a hill, an object loomed in front of them. The object was in the form of a man, about six feet tall with wings on its back.

Becoming frightened, the couples drove away. As they approached a traffic circle near Route 62, they said the thing loomed in front of the car again.

Mallette, 20, said they drove toward Point Pleasant on Route 62 at 100 miles an hour, with the strange creature drifting along behind the car.

The couples said the thing seemed to avoid lights. When they turned into the C. C. Lewis farm, the creature was again in front of the car. What appeared to be a large dead dog was lying on the road.

Later, the couples and police returned to the farm, but the dog had vanished. Deputy Sheriff Millard Halstead searched the TNT area. The deputy said the "thing" was gone, but he found "a strange pile of dust."

Scarberry, 18, said, "Believe me if you ever saw it, you'd be a believer." The men said they might go looking for the thing tonight, but indicated they were afraid they might find it.

Meteor Shower Due In Skies Tonight

CAMBRIDGE, Mass. (AP) — A meteor shower after midnight tonight may produce one of the most spectacular sky shows in more than a century.

The Leonid meteors may flash through the skies about 2 a.m. (EST), toward the east and a little south. Weather, however, could obscure the show.

FIVE DAY FORECAST

Temperatures Thursday through Monday will average 4-8 degrees above normal. Representative normal highs and lows: Cleveland 47-31, Columbus 49-31, Cincinnati 51-35. Not much temperature change until weekend, when it should turn cooler. Precipitation will total .1 to .3 inch as rain or showers about end of week.

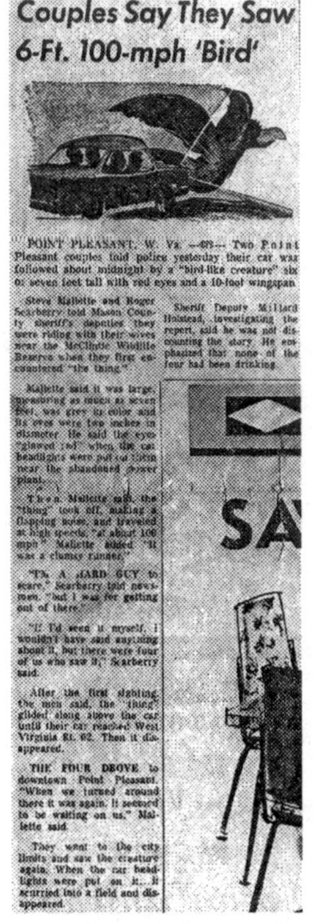

Couples Say They Saw 6-Ft. 100-mph 'Bird'

POINT PLEASANT, W. Va. —(UPI)— Two Point Pleasant couples told police yesterday their car was followed about midnight by a "bird-like creature" six or seven feet tall with red eyes and a 10-foot wingspan.

Steve Mallette and Roger Scarberry told Mason County sheriff's deputies they were riding with their wives near the McClintic Wildlife Reserve when they first encountered "the thing."

Sheriff Deputy Millard Holstead, investigating the report, said he was not discounting the story. He emphasized that none of the four had been drinking.

Mallette said it was large, measuring as much as seven feet, was grey in color and its eyes were two inches in diameter. He said the eyes "glowed red" when the car headlights were put on them near the abandoned power plant.

Then, Mallette said, the "thing" took off, making a flapping noise, and traveled at high speeds, "at about 100 mph," Mallette added. "It was a clumsy runner."

"I'M A HARD GUY to scare," Scarberry told newsmen, "but I was for getting out of there."

"If I'd seen it myself, I wouldn't have said anything about it, but there were four of us who saw it," Scarberry said.

After the first sighting the men said, the "thing" glided along above the car until their car reached West Virginia Rt. 62. Then it disappeared.

THE FOUR DROVE to downtown Point Pleasant. "When we turned around there it was again. It seemed to be waiting on us," Mallette said.

They went to the city limits and saw the creature again. When the car headlights were put on it... it scurried into a field and disappeared.

Couples Say They Saw 6-Ft. 100-mph 'Bird'

POINT PLEASANT, W. Va. —(UPI)— Two Point Pleasant couples told police yesterday their car was followed about midnight by a "bird-like creature" six or seven feet tall with red eyes and a 10-foot wingspan.

Steve Mallette and Roger Scarberry told Mason County sheriff's deputies they were riding with their wives near the McClintic Wildlife Reserve when they first encountered "the thing."

Sheriff Deputy Millard Holstead, investigating the report, said he was not discounting the story. He emphasized that none of the four had been drinking.

Mallette said it was large, measuring as much as seven

Source unknown

Couples Say They Saw 6-Ft. 100-mph 'Bird'

POINT PLEASANT, W. Va. —(AP)— Two Point Pleasant couples told police yesterday their car was followed about midnight by a "bird-like creature" six or seven feet tall with red eyes and a 10-foot wingspan.

Steve Mallette and Roger Scarberry told Mason County sheriff's deputies they were riding with their wives near the McClintic Wildlife Reserve when they first encountered "the thing."

Sheriff Deputy Millard Halstead, investigating the report, said he was not discounting the story. He emphasized that none of the four had been drinking.

Mallette said it was large, measuring as much as seven feet, was grey in color and its eyes were two inches in diameter. He said the eyes "glowed red" when the car headlights were put on them near the abandoned power plant.

Then, Mallette said, the "thing" took off, making a flapping noise, and traveled at high speeds, "at about 100 mph." Mallette added "It was a clumsy runner."

"I'M A HARD GUY to scare," Scarberry told newsmen, "but I was for getting out of there."

"If I'd seen it myself, I wouldn't have said anything about it, but there were four of us who saw it," Scarberry said.

After the first sighting, the men said, the "thing" glided along above the car until their car reached West Virginia Rt. 62. Then it disappeared.

THE FOUR DROVE to downtown Point Pleasant. "When we turned around there it was again. It seemed to be waiting on us," Mallette said.

They went to the city limits and saw the creature again. When the car headlights were put on it, it scurried into a field and disappeared.

Source unknown

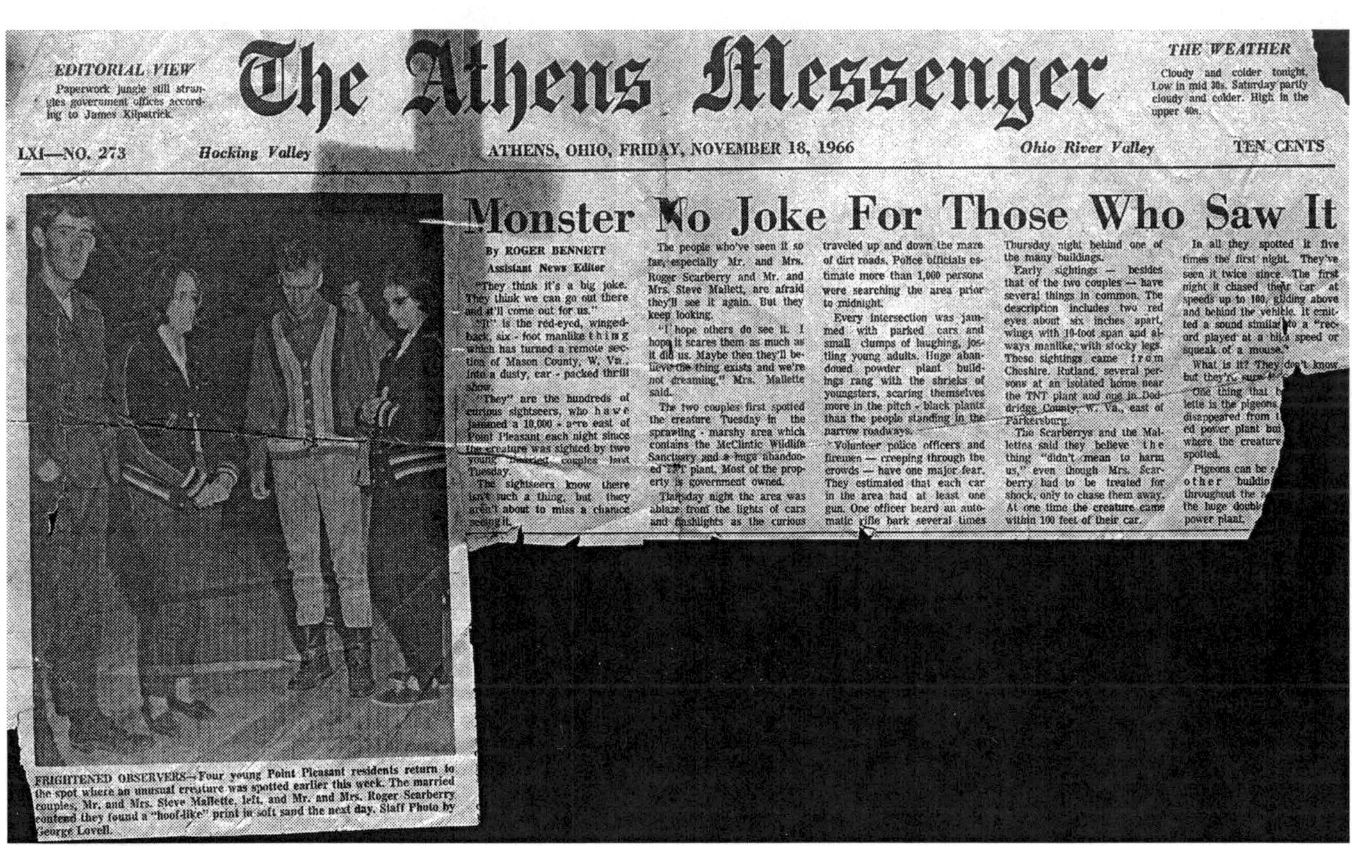

EDITORIAL VIEW

Paperwork jungle still strangles government offices according to James Kilpatrick.

The Athens Messenger

THE WEATHER

Cloudy and colder tonight. Low in mid 30s. Saturday partly cloudy and colder. High in the upper 40s.

LXI—NO. 273 Hocking Valley ATHENS, OHIO, FRIDAY, NOVEMBER 18, 1966 Ohio River Valley TEN CENTS

Monster No Joke For Those Who Saw It

By ROGER BENNETT
Assistant News Editor

"They think it's a big joke. They think we can go out there and it'll come out for us."

"It" is the red-eyed, winged-back, six-foot manlike thing which has turned a remote section of Mason County, W. Va., into a dusty, car-packed thrill show.

"They" are the hundreds of curious sightseers, who have jammed a 10,000-acre east of Point Pleasant each night since the creature was sighted by two young married couples last Tuesday.

The sightseers know there isn't such a thing, but they aren't about to miss a chance seeing it.

The people who've seen it so far, especially Mr. and Mrs. Roger Scarberry and Mr. and Mrs. Steve Mallett, are afraid they'll see it again. But they keep looking.

"I hope others do see it. I hope it scares them as much as it did us. Maybe then they'll believe the thing exists and we're not dreaming," Mrs. Mallette said.

The two couples first spotted the creature Tuesday in the sprawling-marshy area which contains the McClintic Wildlife Sanctuary and a huge abandoned TNT plant. Most of the property is government owned.

Thursday night the area was ablaze from the lights of cars and flashlights as the curious traveled up and down the maze of dirt roads. Police officials estimate more than 1,000 persons were searching the area prior to midnight.

Every intersection was jammed with parked cars and small clumps of laughing, jostling young adults. Huge abandoned powder plant buildings rang with the shrieks of youngsters, scaring themselves more in the pitch-black plants than the people standing in the narrow roadways.

Volunteer police officers and firemen — creeping through the crowds — have one major fear. They estimated that each car in the area had at least one gun. One officer heard an automatic rifle bark several times Thursday night behind one of the many buildings.

Early sightings — besides that of the two couples — have several things in common. The description includes two red eyes about six inches apart, wings with 10-foot span and always manlike, with stocky legs. These sightings came from Cheshire, Rutland, several persons at an isolated home near the TNT plant and one in Doddridge County, W. Va., east of Parkersburg.

The Scarberrys and the Mallettes said they believe the thing "didn't mean to harm us," even though Mrs. Scarberry had to be treated for shock, only to chase them away. At one time the creature came within 100 feet of their car.

In all they spotted it five times the first night. They've seen it twice since. The first night it chased their car at speeds up to 100, gliding above and behind the vehicle. It emitted a sound similar to a "record played at a high speed or squeak of a mouse."

What is it? They don't know but they're sure...

One thing that ... lette is the pigeons ... disappeared from ... ed power plant bu... where the creature ... spotted.

Pigeons can be ... other buildin... throughout the ... the huge doubl... power plant.

FRIGHTENED OBSERVERS—Four young Point Pleasant residents return to the spot where an unusual creature was spotted earlier this week. The married couples, Mr. and Mrs. Steve Mallette, left, and Mr. and Mrs. Roger Scarberry contend they found a "hoof-like" print in soft sand the next day. Staff Photo by George Lovell.

The original witnesses—accompanied by newspaper reporters—returned two days later to the abandoned power plant where they first spotted the Mothman.

EDITORIAL VIEW

Paperwork jungle still strangles government offices according to James Kilpatrick.

The Athe

LXI—NO. 273 *Hocking Valley* ATHENS

Mon

By ROGER
Assistant N

"They think it
They think we c
and it'll come ou
"It" is the re
back, six - foot n
which has turne
tion of Mason C
into a dusty, car
show.
"They" are t
curious sightsee
jammed a 10,000
Point Pleasant e
the creature was
young married
Tuesday.
The sightseer
isn't such a thi
aren't about to
seeing it.

FRIGHTENED OBSERVERS—Four young Point Pleasant residents return to the spot where an unusual creature was spotted earlier this week. The married couples, Mr. and Mrs. Steve Mallette, left, and Mr. and Mrs. Roger Scarberry contend they found a "hoof-like" print in soft sand the next day. Staff Photo by George Lovell.

thens Messen

ATHENS, OHIO, FRIDAY, NOVEMBER 18, 1966

Monster No Joke For Th

By ROGER BENNETT
Assistant News Editor

"They think it's a big joke. They think we can go out there and it'll come out for us."

"It" is the red-eyed, winged-back, six - foot manlike thing which has turned a remote section of Mason County, W. Va., into a dusty, car - packed thrill show.

"They" are the hundreds of curious sightseers, who have jammed a 10,000 - acre east of Point Pleasant each night since the creature was sighted by two young married couples last Tuesday.

The sightseers know there isn't such a thing, but they aren't about to miss a chance seeing it.

The people who've seen it so far, especially Mr. and Mrs. Roger Scarberry and Mr. and Mrs. Steve Mallett, are afraid they'll see it again. But they keep looking.

"I hope others do see it. I hope it scares them as much as it did us. Maybe then they'll believe the thing exists and we're not dreaming," Mrs. Mallette said.

The two couples first spotted the creature Tuesday in the sprawling - marshy area which contains the McClintic Wildlife Sanctuary and a huge abandoned TNT plant. Most of the property is government owned.

Thursday night the area was ablaze from the lights of cars and flashlights as the curious traveled up and down the maze of dirt roads. Police officials estimate more than 1,000 persons were searching the area prior to midnight.

Every intersection was jammed with parked cars and small clumps of laughing, jostling young adults. Huge abandoned powder plant buildings rang with the shrieks of youngsters, scaring themselves more in the pitch - black plants than the people standing in the narrow roadways.

Volunteer police officers and firemen — creeping through the crowds — have one major fear. They estimated that each car in the area had at least one gun. One officer heard an automatic rifle bark several times

THE WEATHER

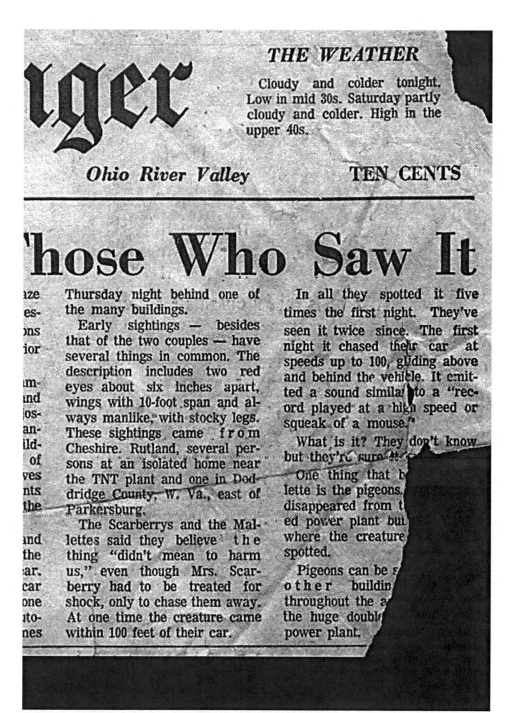

Cloudy and colder tonight. Low in mid 30s. Saturday partly cloudy and colder. High in the upper 40s.

Ohio River Valley TEN CENTS

'hose Who Saw It

ıze
es-
ons
ior

ım-
ınd
ios-
an-
ild-
of
ves
nts
the

ınd
the
ar.
car
one
ıto-
nes

Thursday night behind one of the many buildings.

Early sightings — besides that of the two couples — have several things in common. The description includes two red eyes about six inches apart, wings with 10-foot span and always manlike, with stocky legs. These sightings came from Cheshire, Rutland, several persons at an isolated home near the TNT plant and one in Doddridge County, W. Va., east of Parkersburg.

The Scarberrys and the Mallettes said they believe the thing "didn't mean to harm us," even though Mrs. Scarberry had to be treated for shock, only to chase them away. At one time the creature came within 100 feet of their car.

In all they spotted it five times the first night. They've seen it twice since. The first night it chased their car at speeds up to 100, gliding above and behind the vehicle. It emitted a sound similar to a "record played at a high speed or squeak of a mouse."

What is it? They don't know but they're sure [illegible]

One thing that b
lette is the pigeons.
disappeared from t
ed power plant bu
where the creature
spotted.

Pigeons can be s
other buildin
throughout the a
the huge doubl
power plant.

NO. 141 Phone—461-5000 • COLUMBUS, OHIO 43216, FRIDAY, NOVEMBER 18, 1966 ** Copyright, 1966 The Dispatch Printing Co. 7 Cents

HIGH SCHOOL SCIENCE CLUB SAYS BEAST MAY BE ONE OF ITS WEATHER BALLOONS

Red Eyed 'Winged Monster' Sighted in W. Virginia

POINT PLEASANT, W. Va. (AP)—The Science Interest Club of Proctorville Fairland High School in Lawrence County, Ohio, its adviser says, may have started it all.

"It" being a winged monster with "penetrating red eyes" that has had hundreds stalking the hollows and hills of this Ohio River country the past two nights.

SINCE TUESDAY night numerous calls have besieged the Mason County sheriff's office here telling of "sightings" of the terrifying apparition originally reported by two young Point Pleasant couples.

Whatever it was, authorities say, it left Mr. and Mrs. Steve Mallett and Mr. and Mrs. Roger Scarberry "plenty scared."

The couples said they were riding in a car "about midnight Tuesday" and as their auto crested a hill, "it" loomed in front of them.

THEY SAID IT "resembled a flying man . . . between six and seven feet tall . . . with the wings of an angel, covering a span of about 10 feet . . . gray and white, with penetrating red eyes about six inches apart."

They said they turned tail and headed back from the outlying TNT area (wartime site of a munitions plant) where it appeared. But, according to Mallett, 20, the creature drifted right along behind them as they hit speeds up to 100 miles an hour—and at one point "was in front of the car again."

It veered off as they reached the lights of the city

THEN WEDNESDAY NIGHT, while hundreds — many with weapons—searched the TNT area—a Cheshire, Ohio, man who asked that his name not be used, said "it" chased him near Gallipolis, across the river from here.

Edward Prichard of Huntington, the science club adviser at Proctorville, about 30 miles from here, suggested that balloons released by the club may have been "it."

He said the youngsters, conducting studies on air currents, released two 4 by 7 foot gas-filled balloons.

"THE PREVAILING winds would carry them over Mason County," Prichard said. "Light catches these things in strange ways at some angles. Imagination can do the rest."

NO. 141 Phone—461-5000 • COLUMBUS, OHIO 43216, FRI

HIGH SCHOOL SCIENCE CLUB SAYS BEAST

Red Eyed 'Winged Monste

POINT PLEASANT, W. Va. (AP)—The Science Interest Club of Proctorville Fairland High School in Lawrence County, Ohio, its adviser says, may have started it all.

"It" being a winged monster with "penetrating red eyes" that has had hundreds stalking the hollows and hills of this Ohio River country the past two nights.

SINCE TUESDAY night numerous calls have besieged the Mason County sheriff's office here telling of "sightings" of the terrifying apparition originally reported by two young Point Pleasant couples.

Whatever it was, authorities say, it left Mr. and Mrs. Steve Mallett and Mr. and Mrs. Roger Scarberry "plenty scared."

The couples said they were riding in a car "about midnight Tuesday" and as their auto crested a hill, "it" loomed in front of them.

THEY SAID IT "resembled a flying man . . . between six and seven feet tall . . . with the wings of an angel, covering a span of about 10 feet . . . gray and white, with penetrating red eyes about six inches apart."

They said they turned tail and headed back from

IDAY, NOVEMBER 18, 1966 ** Copyright, 1966 The Dispatch Printing Co. 7 Cents

MAY BE ONE OF ITS WEATHER BALLOONS

er' Sighted in W. Virginia

the outlying TNT area (wartime site of a munitions plant) where it appeared. But, according to Mallett, 20, the creature drifted right along behind them as they hit speeds up to 100 miles an hour—and at one point "was in front of the car again."

It veered off as they reached the lights of the city

THEN WEDNESDAY NIGHT, while hundreds — many with weapons—searched the TNT area—a Cheshire, Ohio, man who asked that his name not be used, said "it" chased him near Gallipolis, across the river from here.

Edward Prichard of Huntington, the science club adviser at Proctorville, about 30 miles from here, suggested that balloons released by the club may have been "it."

He said the youngsters, conducting studies on air currents, released two 4 by 7 foot gas-filled balloons.

"THE PREVAILING winds would carry them over Mason County," Prichard said. "Light catches these things in strange ways at some angles. Imagination can do the rest."

Use Force, U.K. Urged

U.N. HITS RHODESIA

'Red-Eyed Creature' Reported in W. Va.

POINT PLEASANT, W.Va. (UPI)—Two Point Pleasant couples told police Wednesday their car was followed about midnight by a "birdlike creature" 6 to 7 feet tall with red eyes and a 10-foot wingspan.

Steve Mallette and Roger Scarberry and their wives told Mason County sheriff's deputies they were riding near the McClintic Wildlife Reserve when they first encountered "the thing."

Mallette said it was large, measuring as much as 7 feet, was grey in color with eyes two inches in diameter. He said the eyes "glowed red" when the car headlights were put on them near an abandoned power plant.

Then, Mallette said, the "thing" took off, marking a flapping noise, and traveled at high speeds, "at about 100 miles an hour." Mallette added, "it was a clumsy runner."

Scarberry said, "If I'd seen it only by myself, I wouldn't have said anything about it, but there were four of us who saw it."

Vol. 22, No. 322 Saturday, Nov. 19, 1966

UNITED NATIONS, N.Y. (AP) — The U.N. General Assembly overwhelmingly urged Britain Thursday to use force if necessary to end the Rhodesian rebellion.

The assembly approved 89 to 2 a 53-nation resolution calling on Britain "to take all necessary measures, including, in particular, the use of force" to overthrow the breakaway, minority regime of Ian D. Smith.

Portugal and South Africa cast the two negative votes. The resolution condemned the two nations for their support of the Smith regime.

The force of the resolution was

American troops in Vietnam read about the first Mothman sighting three days after it happened.

'Red-Eyed Creature' Reported in W. Va.

POINT PLEASANT, W.Va. (UPI)—Two Point Pleasant couples told police Wednesday their car was followed about midnight by a "birdlike creature" 6 to 7 feet tall with red eyes and a 10-foot wingspan.

Steve Mallette and Roger Scarberry and their wives told Mason County sheriff's deputies they were riding near the McClintic Wildlife Reserve when they first encountered "the thing."

Mallette said it was large, measuring as much as 7 feet, was grey in color with eyes two inches in diameter. He said the eyes "glowed red" when the car headlights were put on them near an abandoned power plant.

Then, Mallette said, the "thing" took off, marking a flapping noise, and traveled at high speeds, "at about 100 miles an hour." Mallette added, "it was a clumsy runner."

Scarberry said, "If I'd seen it only by myself, I wouldn't have said anything about it, but there were four of us who saw it."

Our 'Bird' Has Law On Its Side

Register Nov. 19, 1966

If Mason County's "bird" should prove to be a Sandhill Crane, as suggested by Dr. Robert Smith of the West Virginia University Biology Department, then the law is on its side to provide protection.

Officials note that migratory birds of all kinds are protected by federal and state wildlife laws.

Millard Halstead, Mason County Sheriff's Deputy, said Friday, he had been in contact with Dr. Smith and from a comparison of descriptions feels that the "bird man" might be a Sandhill Crane. The bird stands five to six feet tall, has about an 80-inch wing spread and has patches of red around its eyes.

Halstead said the bird is extremely rare, and he understands there are only 30 of them left in this country.

Sheriff George Johnson said he would arrest any persons caught in the TNT area with a loaded gun after dark. There were earlier reports of armed people roaming the area. Johnson has asked that residents not harm the bird.

Haunting Creature Seen Twice

POINT PLEASANT — Mason County may be loosing one of its recent tourist attractions.

Two Sunday sightings indicate the strange flying creature which has been spotted several times at the old TNT plant, near Point Pleasant, may be leaving his happy haunting grounds.

Miss Connie Jo Carpenter, 18, New Haven, saw the "awful looking creature" flying toward her car on Route 33, near New Haven, about 10:30 a.m. She said the thing was "man-like, with a big wing span."

She said she tromped on the gas and didn't look back to see if the thing followed.

Later Sunday night, two young girls reported seeing a similar man-like creature on Route 60, near St. Albans. The two young girls, walking home from a store, ran to a neighbors home. The neighbor confirmed the sighting.

The girls said the flying creature had "big red pop-eyes and didn't have a beak." St. Albans is about 40 miles south of Point Pleasant.

Source unknown

NIGHT RIDER IN SKY AFRAID OF LIGHTS

People in Mason County are talking about a flying man who is afraid of lights.

He is a 6-foot creature with a wingspan of 10 feet and can scoot along at 100 miles an hour.

Wednesday about midnight the gray and white replacement to mundane flying saucers startled two young couples driving north of Point Pleasant on W. Va. 62, they said.

Once they spotted it, they headed for town at 100 miles an hour and along came their weird airborne friend, breezing about 50 feet above them with the greatest of ease, they told police.

But once they neared the lighted confines of the town, the high horsepowered night rider in the sky veered around and took off toward the dark and less populous countryside—the two couples told police.

Source unknown

Four More Claim Seeing Big Red-Eyed Bird

POINT PLEASANT, W. Va. — (UPI) — The mystery of the flying "whatever it was" continued here today.

Four more people reported seeing a huge, bird-like creature with red eyes. A farmer also said his German Shepherd chased something "with red reflectors" and then vanished.

Source unknown

Is Mysterious Creature Balloon Or Crane?

POINT PLEASANT — Rumors are flying through Mason County faster than the "thing," which has been spotted by several people in various locations.

The "thing" is described as being six feet tall, soars with a pair of wings with a 10-foot span, has red eyes six inches apart and leaves a print like a hoof mark.

Two young married couples first spotted the "thing" Tuesday night in a 10,000-acre section east of Point Pleasant. The sector contains the McClintic Wildlife Sanctuary and an abandoned government TNT plant.

Since that time the flying creature has been seen in various parts of West Virginia and Ohio. Each description contains the phrase "red eyes, six inches apart."

The "thing" has caused a sudden interest in the remote TNT plant area and nightly motorists plow bumper-to-bumper over the dusty, dirt roads in hopes of spotting the creature.

Monday morning quarterbacks have taken three approaches to the sightings. They either laugh at the sighters, give theories about the creature or they contend they've seen it themselves.

The latest theory about the creature was advanced by Dr. Robert Smith, associate professor of biology at West Virginia University. Smith said the descriptions of the creature fit that of the huge sandhill crane.

Smith said the crane stands six feet or better, has a huge wing span and has red forehead feathers.

However, Ohio University Zoology department officials gave a different view concerning the sandhill crane theory.

Ohio U. officials said there has never been a known sighting of a sandhill crane in this part of the country.

In his book, "The Sandhill Cranes," Lawrence H. Walkinshaw, says the crane normally inhabits the plains of … and the flat country o… Michigan, Minnesota, … sin and the Dakotas.

The birds migrate e… to the Gulf Coast, bu… grate down the Mississippi Valley. Like some other birds, the crane migrates at night.

The sandhill crane is grey-brown in color and has a red forehead.

Members of the Proctorville-Fairland High School Science Interest Club have another theory. Students of the Lawrence County school say the creature could be one of the two gas filled balloons they've released to study air currents.

The 4 x 7 balloons were released about 30 miles west of … poke," a member of the heron family.

Others contend the creature could be one of the wild geese, which live on the ponds of the wildlife sanctuary. The geese stand about two and a half to three feet tall.

One man said the description fit his "mother-in-law exactly, especially the red eyes, six inches apart."

Another Point Pleasant man said the creature is something from the moon, chased down to earth by recent moon launch-…

…es who first …fr. and Mrs. …nd Mr. and …e, disagreed …heory about the sandhill crane.

After viewing a picture of the bird, one of them commented, "My God, that's not the thing we saw. This thing could never chase us as it did."

Mrs. Mallette said, "I just wish Dr. Smith could see the thing."

The "thing" appeared in a road near an abandoned power plant at the TNT facility. The four spotted the "thing" five different times as it chased them at speeds of 100 miles an hour toward Point Pleasant.

One thing for certain, the remote, lonely roads in the TNT area aren't suited for late night astronomy studies now and the sweethearts of the area are up in arms.

THE MESSENGER, Sunday, Nov. 20, 1966 – Page D-1

SANDHILL CRANE—A West Virginia University associate professor contends the mysterious creature being seen in Mason County could be a sandhill crane. The crane has never been seen in this area, officials said.

THE MESSENGER, Sunday, Nov. 20, 1966 – Page D-1

SANDHILL CRANE—A West Virginia University associate professor contends the mysterious creature being seen in Mason County could be a sandhill crane. The crane has never been seen in this area, officials said.

Almost immediately after the initial sightings, many opinions began to surface about just what the witnesses saw (or didn't see.)

Is Mysterious Creature Balloon Or Crane?

POINT PLEASANT — Rumors are flying through Mason County faster than the "thing," which has been spotted by several people in various locations.

The "thing" is described as being six feet tall, soars with a pair of wings with a 10-foot span, has red eyes six inches apart and leaves a print like a hoof mark.

Two young married couples first spotted the "thing" Tuesday night in a 10,000-acre section east of Point Pleasant. The sector contains the McClintic Wildlife Sanctuary and an abandoned government TNT plant.

Since that time the flying creature has been seen in various parts of West Virginia and Ohio. Each description contains the phrase "red eyes, six inches apart."

The "thing" has caused a sudden interest in the remote TNT plant area and nightly motorists plow bumper-to-bumper over the dusty, dirt roads in hopes of spotting the creature.

Monday morning quarterbacks have taken three approaches to the sightings. They either laugh at the sighters, give theories about the creature or they contend they've seen it themselves.

The latest theory about the creature was advanced by Dr. Robert Smith, associate professor of biology at West Virginia University. Smith said the descriptions of the creature fit that of the huge sandhill crane.

Smith said the crane stands six feet or better, has a huge wing span and has red forehead feathers.

However, Ohio University Zoology department officials gave a different view concerning the sandhill crane theory.

Ohio U. officials said there has never been a known sighting of a sandhill crane in this part of the country.

In his book, "The Sandhill Cranes," Lawrence H. Walkinshaw, says the crane normally inhabits the plains of [illegible] and the flat country o[illegible] Michigan, Minnesota, [illegible] sin and the Dakotas.

The birds migrate e[illegible] to the Gulf Coast. bu[illegible] grate down the Mississippi Valley. Like some other birds, the crane migrates at night.

The sandhill crane is grey-brown in color and has a red forehead.

Members of the Proctorville-Fairland High School Science Interest Club have another theory. Students of the Lawrence County school say the creature could be one of the two gas filled balloons they've released to study air currents.

The 4 x 7 balloons were released about 30 miles west of [illegible] poke," a member of the heron family.

Others contend the creature could be one of the wild geese, which live on the ponds of the wildlife sanctuary. The geese stand about two and a half to three feet tall.

One man said the description fit his "mother-in-law exactly, especially the red eyes, six inches apart."

Another Point Pleasant man said the creature is something from the moon, chased down to earth by recent moon launch-[illegible]

[illegible]es who first [illegible] Mr. and Mrs. [illegible]nd Mr. and [illegible]e, disagreed [illegible]heory about the sandhill crane.

After viewing a picture of the bird, one of them commented, "My God, that's not the thing we saw. This thing could never chase us as it did."

Mrs. Mallette said, "I just wish Dr. Smith could see the thing."

The "thing" appeared in a road near an abandoned power plant at the TNT facility. The four spotted the "thing" five different times as it chased them at speeds of 100 miles an hour toward Point Pleasant.

One thing for certain, the remote, lonely roads in the TNT area aren't suited for late night astronomy studies now and the sweethearts of the area are up in arms.

Monster Returns To Mason

By MARY HYRE
Point Pleasant Correspondent

POINT PLEASANT — Six — or maybe seven — more people became believers in the Mason County Monster Wednesday night.

What is it they saw? They don't know, but they have managed to convince a raft of people they saw something.

The latest observers of the red-eyed, wing-backed six-foot thing are Mr. and Mrs. Raymond Wamsley; Ricky, Connie and Vickie Thomas and Marcella Bennett.

They spotted the monster around 9 p. m. Wednesday outside the home of Mr. and Mrs. Ralph Thomas, in the TNT area, where the thing was sighted Tuesday night.

Observer number seven is reported to be a Cheshire area youth who allegedly was chased by a thing matching the description of the Mason County Monster. The chase took place on Route 7 in Ohio.

Wednesday night's sighting took place as the Wamsley's and the Thomas children were leaving the Thomas home. They said the red-eyed creature was lying on the road behind a car.

... the house and called police. Later they ventured outside and spotted the creature watching them while partially hidden behind a pile of bricks. They said the creature then flew away.

At the time of the spotting, officers and fire department volunteers were searching near an old power plant in the TNT area, where the monster was first spotted Tuesday night by two young couples.

Mr. and Mrs. Steve Mallette and Mr. and Mrs. Roger Scarberry said the thing chased their car at speeds up to 100 miles an hour around midnight Tuesday.

Officers said the TNT area was flooded with curious sightseers Wednesday night. One motorist reported his children "wanted to see it right now."

Several people reported they had to take their children out because "they about drove us mad wanting to see it."

One man contended it was something caused by the U. S. space program. He said, "You see, it's that talk of going to the moon and that stuff. It's hard to tell what they've caused to come back to earth."

Mrs. Thomas, who was at church during Wednesday night's sighting, said she had a vision Monday night that a creature would appear. In the vision, she said, the creature would frighten people, but not harm anyone.

Pacific Stars & Stripes 20 Nov [illegible] 66

4 More Say They Saw Red-Eyed 'Whatever'

POINT PLEASANT, W.Va. (UPI) — The mystery of the flying "whatever it was" continued here Thursday.

Four more persons reported seeing a huge, bird-like creature with red eyes, and in Doddridge County, more than 100 miles to the north, a farmer feels his german shepherd was "dognaped" by the thing.

Mason County Sheriff George Johnson said he does not discount the stories of Steve Mallette and Roger Scarberry and their wives. All four swear they saw the creature three times late Tuesday and early Wednesday, near an abandoned power plant five miles north of here.

Raymond Wamsley and his wife, and Marcella Bennett and Ricky Thomas told Johnson they saw it, too, in the same general area.

Johnson said he feels whatever everyone saw was nothing more than a "freak shitepoke," a large bird of the heron family. The shitepoke, or shag as it is sometimes known, is the smallest heron in the western hemisphere.

No one, however, could explain how a shag or similar large bird could fly 100 m.p.h. as Scarberry and Mallette said the thing they saw did. All four said they would take lie detector tests.

At a farm in Doddridge County near the Harrison County community of Salem, contractor Newell Partridge said he saw something with eyes like "red reflectors" in a meadow near his home. He sighted this "thing" about 90 minutes before the Point Pleasant incident.

Partridge said his television set began acting up, "sounding like a generator," and his $350 german shepherd, Bandit, started "carrying on something terrible."

After the dog had howled for some time, Partridge said, he opened the door and shone a flashlight into the field where the "reflectors" were seen.

The dog's hair stood straight up, Partridge [illegible] and the animal then went after the r[illegible]. The dog never returned, and [illegible] it was found.

Partridge a[illegible] wife said the dog had never stayed [illegible] from home for more than 15 minutes in the last three years.

'Bird' Gets

Robert L. Smith, associate professor of wildlife management at West Virginia University, has given "bird stories" the business in his weekly column for the Morgantown Dominion-Post.

A copy of his column was offered The Register by R. Ivan Pinnell, police reporter for the Morgantown Post who said "the article appeared in our paper as a result of the sighting of a bird similar to that seen in Mason County."

Pinnell said "the Monongalia County bird had one difference-it had large green eyes." He noted that Monongalia Sheriff Charles J. Whiston feels the bird there is "a hoax." He said it was only seen once, about two days "after your bird was sighted."

Professor Smith, who previously informed the Mason County Sheriff's Office that the "bird" here probably was a sandhill crane, wrote as folfows:

"This week I had planned to write about venison, more specifically on the care and handling of the deer carcass. But instead I am going to write about the sandhill crane, simply to set the record straight about the "monster" bird that made the headline in Mason County. Much of the information has been misinterperted, added to, substracted and changed with the telling. The releases were beautiful examples of how a

POINT PLEASANT REGISTER,

—1—

nia to New England, but it disappeared from eastern United States many years ago. It is now essentially a bird of midwestern and western North America, where it feeds to low wet ground and marshes where it nests.

"The sandhill crane breeds from Siberia, Alaska and northern Canada south to Florida, Cuba, southern Mississippi, Nebraska, Arizona and northern California. It winters in southern Georgia, the Gulf Coast and California south to southern Mexico and Cuba.

"This bird has been known to nest as far east as Ohio. There are several records of migrants in southwestern Pennsylvania. The bird was sighted some years ago in West Virginia, but there is no official record since the bird was never collected. The bird at McClintic Wildlife Station is probably a migrant that has strayed somewhat off course.

A great deal of misinformation has circulated about the rarity of the bird. It is a rare bird in West Virginia, but as species the sandhill crane is in no immediate danger of extinction. Several races the Florida sandhill crane, the Cuban sandhill crane and the migratory greater sandhill crane are greatly reduced in numbers; but a fourth race, the lesser sandhill, is relatively abundant. In fact in southern Canada and in the Dakotas, as well as in New Mexico and Texas, sandhill crane have caused serious crop damage. Sandhill crane counts in southern New

Once-Over

story can change with each retelling.

"There is no doubt in my mind that the "strange monster" or "large terrifying bird" or what have you was a sandhill crane. The identification was rather easy from the descriptions of the bird in the news releases.

"The sandhill crane is a large bird, standing four to 4½ feet tall. Its stance is rather erect, and it walks with a strong deliberate stride that seen in the dark might vaguely suggest a human. The bird is blue-gray in color except for the bare-red colored skin on the forehead and crown. Under the glare of headlights the reflection of the eyes and the roundish red patches on the head would leave the impression of two large red eyes. Startled, the bird might have extended its wings which with its upright posture could account for the description of "wings like an angel's."

"The bird has a wingspread of about seven feet, yet in spite of its size it weights only about eight pounds. Most highly exaggerated was its speed of flight, supposedly around 100 miles an hour. With a real strong tail wind, the bird might do 50; the actual flight speed is probably much closer to 30.

"At one time the sandhill crane occurred as a breeding bird or migrant from Califor-

SEE STORY NO. 1 PAGE 3

sandhill crane have caused serious crop damage. Sandhill crane counts in southern New Mexico and Texas alone yielded around 150,000 birds in 1960. That year the Fish and Wildlife Service held an experimental hunting season on the crane, highly esteemed as a game and table bird.

"Somewhere along the way, the sandhill crane became confused with the whooping crane, the rare white-colored species of which some 45, not 30, individuals still live in the wild.

"The food of the sandhill crane is chiefly vegetable matter: roots, tubers grain, grass and seeds. It is fond of corn, sorghum, potatoes and alfalfa. The cranes will also take mice, crayfish, frogs and insects at opportune times.

"In the past week the crane seems to have acquired a reputation as a dog killer. Undoubtedly the bird with its long

tedly the bird with its long sharp bill is capable of inflicing injury on if not actually killing a dog. But this doesn not mean that the bird did kill a dog and it certainly couldn't carry the animal anyplace. The only conditions under which the crane would attack dog or man are when the bird is wounded or held at bay. Then it can be dangerous. In recent years no stories along this line have circulated. But Audubon and Edward Forbush both relate incidents of being pursued by wounded birds.

"The experience of the past two weeks is an example of how sighting of an unfamiliar animal seen under unusual circumstances can soon be blown out of all proportion to the actual situation. It also points out how some of our most mysterious observations have rather simple explanations."

Register No. 21

'Bird' Echoes Still

Calls, letters and rumors continue to plague the Mason County Sheriff's office from persons offering information on the so-called "bird" that was spotted in Mason County last Tuesday night.

However, the original four persons who reported their exprience to Deputy Sheriff Millard Halstead, are not convinced that the creature is a bird.

Dr. Robert Smith of the West Virginia University biology department said the description fits that of a Sandhill Crane, but Mr. and Mrs. Steve Mallette and Mr. and Mrs. Roger Scarberry contend that the creature they saw around midnight Tuesday, had the shape more like that of a man, but had a wide wing spread and red eyes.

Meanwhile, Sheriff Halstead said four other persons said they saw the creature Saturday night on the Camp Conley Road about one mile back from the main highway or State Route 62.

Four youths, Billy Burdette, 16; Darrell Love, 18; Johnny Love, 14, and John Morrow, 14, all of Point Pleasant Route 2 described it as having red eyes and said when they got close to it, it flew off.

Hundreds of sightseers have toured the TNT area since the report by local news media Wednesday, but during the weekend traffic tampered off some after some authorities labeled it as a Sandhill Crane.

Sheriff Halstead said today, he had received two letters from persons across the country who were offering information in an attempt to identify it.

A Silver Springs, Md., resident Henry J. Frey said he had read the account in the Washington Daily News. Frey said he is "an authority on many subjects" and has concluded from the description that it is a Great Blue Heron. He said these birds belong to a family of wandering birds.

Halstead received another letter from Donald Birchfield, who lives in Altoona, Pa., and had picked it up in a local paper. He is of the opinion that it is a Sandhill Crane.,

It was also reported the Sandhill Crane has a bigger population than 30 as reported earlier.

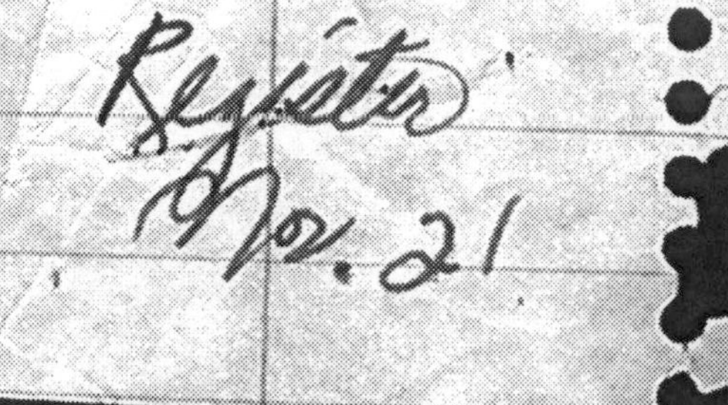

Register No. 21

'Bird' Echoes Still

Calls, letters and rumors continue to plague the Mason County Sheriff's office from persons offering information on the so-called "bird" that was spotted in Mason County last Tuesday night.

However, the original four persons who reported their exprience to Deputy Sheriff Millard Halstead, are not convinced that the creature is a bird.

Dr. Robert Smith of the West Virginia University biology department said the description fits that of a Sandhill Crane, but Mr. and Mrs. Steve Mallette and Mr. and Mrs. Roger Scarberry contend that the creature they saw around midnight Tuesday, had the shape more like that of a man, but had a wide wing spread and red eyes.

Meanwhile, Sheriff Halstead said four other persons said they saw the creature Saturday night on the Camp Conley Road about one mile back from the main highway or State Route 62.

Four youths, Billy Burdette, 16; Darrell Love, 18; Johnny Love, 14, and John Morrow, 14, all of Point Pleasant Route 2 described it as having red eyes and said when they got close to it, it flew off.

Hundreds of sightseers have toured the TNT area since the report by local news media Wednesday, but during the weekend traffic tampered off some after some authorities labeled it as a Sandhill Crane.

Sheriff Halstead said today, he had received two letters from persons across the country who were offering information in an attempt to identify it.

A Silver Springs, Md., resident Henry J. Frey said he had read the account in the Washington Daily News. Frey said he is "an authority on many subjects" and has concluded from the description that it is a Great Blue Heron. He said these birds belong to a family of wandering birds.

Halstead received another letter from Donald Birchfield, who lives in Altoona, Pa., and had picked it up in a local paper. He is of the opinion that it is a Sandhill Crane.,

It was also reported the Sandhill Crane has a bigger population than 30 as reported earlier.

© *The Point Pleasant Register*, Point Pleasant, WV. Reprinted by permission.

8 Witnesses Now Testifying To Seeing Flying Creature

POINT PLEASANT, W. Va. (UPI)—Eight people say they saw a flying creature near this Ohio River community, a dog could have fallen victim to "it," and now a Kanawha County gravedigger saw a "brown man" fly past him last weekend.

Kenneth Duncan of Blue Creek near Charleston said he and some other men were digging his brother-in-law's grave on Saturday when something that "looked like a brown human being" buzzed past.

"It was gliding through the trees and was in sight for about a minute," Duncan said. Four other men helping to dig the grave didn't see it.

The "thing," described as a huge bird - like creature with eyes like "red reflectors" and a wing span of 10 feet, first was reported to police by Steve Mallette and Roger Scarberry and their wives yho said they saw it three times late Tuesday and early Wednesday about five miles north of here.

Four other persons also told Mason County Sheriff George Johnson they saw it in the same general area.

And a contractor, Newell Partridge, who lives 100 miles to the north, said he feels it may have had something to do with the disappearance of his $350 German shepherd dog, Bandit.

Partridge said he sighted the "thing" in a meadow near his home in Doddridge County about 90 minutes before the Point Pleasant sightings.

Partridge said his television set "began acting like a generator" and Bandit "started carrying on something terrible."

Partridge said he shined a flashlight into the field and saw something with eyes like "red reflectors." The dog's hair stood straight up, he said, and the animal went into the field.

The dog never returned, Partridge said, and there was no trace of it in the morning.

Johnson said he was not discounting the stories he was told but said he feels what was seen was nothing more than a "freak shitepoke," a large bird of the heron family.

The shitepoke, sometimes called a shag, is the smallest heron in the Western Hemisphere. Officials were at a loss, however, to explain how a shag could fly at 100 miles per hour as Scarberry and Mallette said the creature did.

Says 'It' is Sandhill Crane

Dr. Robert Smith, West Virginia University, informed Mason County Sheriff's Department this morning that "The Bird" or "Thing" reported seen by at least eight persons during the past three nights in his opinion is a Sand Hill Crane, found generally in Florida, Georgia, the Mississippi Valley, and northward to Manatoba.

Dr. Smith said the "monster" doesn't really have big red eyes—that it has red feathers around the eyes, 80-inch wing spread, and it does stand six feet or better.

Dr. Smith said it would not attack humans, unless provoked. It is mainly a vegetarian. He added, "It does have a large bill, and could kill a dog but would not eat it."

Dr. Smith will send officials a sketch of the big bird.

Excitement Dying Down:

Mysterious 'Mothman' Said Still at Large

POINT PLEASANT, W.Va. (AP) — The mysterious mothman was still at large near this normally quiet Ohio River community, but the excitement he caused is dying down.

The excitement began two weeks ago when Mr. and Mrs. Roger Scarberry and Mr. and Mrs. Steve Mallett, all of Point Pleasant, spotted a large white apparition flying at high speed, following their car.

They told a deputy sheriff it looked like "a flying man with 10 foot wings." They said it was about seven feet tall with large red eyes.

These reports brought curious crowds to the McClintic Wildlife Station where the incident occurred. Volunteer fire department members had to help keep traffic moving.

During the next three days at least eight persons reported various similar creatures. On Nov. 18 two volunteer firemen, Capt. Paul Yoder and Benjamin Enochs, said they saw what definitely was a very large bird with large red eyes.

Dr. Robert L. Smith, associate professor of wildlife biology at WVU, said the descriptions all fitted the sandhill crane, the second largest American crane, which stands almost as high as a man and has a wingspan of more than seven feet.

Bird, Plane Or Batman?

Mason Countians Hunt 'Moth Man'

By PAT SILER

POINT PLEASANT—Sighters clogged the roads north here Wednesday night as ason countians flocked to a desolate TNT area to join search for the "Monster lan."

...'s deputies reported ...o couples told them ...hey had sighted the ...ure" Tuesday night ...e old powerhouse, five miles from Point Pleasant.

It has been variously described as a flying man with a ten-foot wingspread capable of pursuing cars at 100 miles per hour, and as a huge gray and white bird "with wings like an angel and legs like a man, seven feet tall with two large, red eyes about six inches apart.

Officials at the McClintock Wildlife Station said no such description can be found in any of their fowl manuals. They did suggest, however, that it is geese migrating time, and that flights have been sighted in the area.

But Mr. and Mrs. Roger Scarberry, and Mr. and Mrs Steve Mallett maintain that the "thing" followed their car Tuesday night, zig-zagging in front of the auto as it speeded along W. Va. 62.

The men told deputies the creature veered away as the car approached the Point Pleasant city limits.

The volunteer fire department was called to assist Wednesday night in traffic duty at the scene of the "fly-over."

One fireman commented: "It looks like Mason County fair time."

Not correct - bird never did appear in front of car.

Source unknown

Creature Seen Near Appleseed Park

NELSONVILLE — Four Nelsonville women returning Wednesday night from work at the Logan Goodyear plant were quite shaken when a huge bird nearly collided with their car near the Johnny Appleseed Roadside Park, near the Athens-Hocking County line on Route 33.

From their description, the bird is similar to a creature which has been sighted in the vicinity of Point Pleasant for several weeks.

Dixie Auflick was driving the car. Passengers were Edna Guess, Betty Hook and Kathleen Bond, all Goodyear employes.

The incident occurred sometime between 11 and 11:30 p.m.

Mrs. Guess said they had stopped at the park to close a car door which had been not tightly latched. They traveled a few hundred feet from the park when the bird swooped in front of the car from the right.

There is a small swamp area between the highway and the railroad, extending to the Hocking River.

Mrs. Guess said the bird barely skimmed over the top of the car and could be seen clearly. It had large red eyes. The body was described as "brownish and silvery." Another smaller bird followed close behind, they said.

A youth in Haydenville reportedly saw a similar bird near that community early last week.

Mason County's 'Bird' Known 'Far And Wide'

Mason County's "Bird" story has made its way into newspapers all across the land and just last week turned up in the Army's official publication of the Stars and Stripes.

In the November 19 Pacific edition a two-column headline "Red-Eyed Creature Reported in W. Va." drew the attention of many servicemen in Viet Nam.

Among those was a regular army man from Point Pleasant, Sgt 1st cl-E 7 Morton A. Jackson. He mailed the front page of the paper to his mother, Mrs. Roy Jackson and sister, Mrs. Millard Halstead, both of Point Pleasant.

The Sergeant, who is a brother-in-law to Deputy Sheriff Millard Halstead, had not received any information concerning this when he spotted the release in the Army's paper.

However Mrs Jackson of 2319 Jefferson Ave. said they since had mailed clippings of circumstances surrounding it to her son.

Sgt. Jackson mailed his letter home from Viet Nam on November 21 and it was received here Friday morning.

The serviceman's address is Sgt. 1st cl-E 7 Morton A. Jackson, RA 35653076, U. S. A. STRAT CON Fac. Phu Lan, San Francisco, Calif. 96243.

At the same time, Lt. Col. William L. Latta Jr. in Viet Nam sent two articles from Stars and Stripes about "the bird", with the note: "Even Point Pleasant gets in the news in the Pacific."

The clippings were received here by Colonel Latta's wife, Pauline Stephenson Latta of Columbus, O., and were forwarded to The Register.

The Register has received requests for newspapers containing "bird" articles from various places, including Arkansas.

Lights, Circular Objects Athens Messenger - 12-12-66

Cheshire People Tell Of Strange Sightings

By MARY HYRE
Point Pleasant Correspondent

CHESHIRE — Strange objects have been seen in the Cheshire area during the past several weeks, but witnesses have been reluctant to talk about the sightings. Sunday night, however, several revealed their stories.

Mrs. Roy Grose, Cheshire, said that she was awakened by the barking of her dog at 4:45 a.m., Nov. 17. She got up to see what was wrong.

The moon was shining very brightly that night, she said, and when she looked out the kitchen window, she saw a bright-colored circular object on the other side of Route 7.

The saucer - shaped object, Mrs. Grose went on, was the size of a small house with what looked like sections or compartments of blue and red windows.

The object was over an open field at about housetop level, she said, and its brilliant lights were visible for about 30 or 40 seconds before it zigzagged and suddenly disappeared.

As she was watching the object, Mrs. Grose said that she was afraid to call the rest of the family because it might have left by the time they got back to the window. In describing her feelings of that morning, the housewife and piano teacher said only, "I was stunned."

On the other side of town, Charles Hern, an employe at the Kyger Creek Power Plant, took his dog out for a walk along the Ohio River at about 6:30 a.m. last Thursday morning.

He noticed a red light across the river. At first he thought it was only a trapper in a boat checking his muskrat traps, but as he looked he realized that it was something he had never seen before, he said.

He called his wife, and together they saw that the light was on the shore. It appeared, they said, that little people were going to and from the object.

Mrs. Hern said that they were so stunned and dazzled that they decided to call their neighbors, Mr. and Mrs. Walter Taylor.

Mrs. Taylor, a school teacher, was the first to come outside, and she, too, saw the red and orange lights shining from the object by the river. She said that one of the lights was directed toward the water part of the time. Taylor, who arrived at the scene soon after his wife, collaborated with the other witnesses.

Although the others went back inside, Mrs. Hern remained outside for awhile. The lights went out she said, and then lights of another color appeared. Then, she said, the object went straight up and vanished.

Hern said, "I've lived on this river bank since I was 12 years old and I know every boat light, but this definitely was something I've never seen before."

A high school student reportedly saw an object of a similar description south of there at about 5 a.m. that same morning.

A George Creek woman reported that she was traveling along George Creek Road at about 7 p.m. Friday evening with her four children when they saw a redish orange metalic object just above a utility pole. It was the size of a helicopter, she said, adding that it definitely was not one.

She said that it moved along the highway in front of the car for about a mile, disappearing as it approached the brighter lights of the power transformers.

The sightings were near the area where a large bird-like creature has been reported in recent weeks.

John A. Keel, a magazine writer from New York City, has been in the area since Wednesday collecting material on both the UFO and creature sightings. He said that the sightings are similar to others throughout the United States.

Mystery Bird Seen Flying Over Avenue

POINT PLEASANT — It looked like a bird as big as a plane and had legs like a man, the latest Mason Monster sighter reported.

Mrs. Mabel McDaniel of 30th Street, Point Pleasant, said she saw a dark-colored flying creature with an extremely wide wingspan as she was driving on Jackson Avenue at about 5 p.m. Wednesday.

Mrs. McDaniel is the mother of Mrs. Roger Scarberry, one of the original sighters of the bird-like creature popularly known as the "Mason Monster."

A number of hunters have reported seeing owls, larger than normal size, in the Mason County area.

Athens Messenger - Dec. 13-66 (was seen Dec. 11-66)

'Creature' Seen Again Flying Over TNT Area

POINT PLEASANT — Chester Leport, Point Pleasant, and Stevie Pearson Jr., 13, Point Pleasant Route 1, saw a strange object gliding over the TNT area Sunday about 3:30 p.m.

Leport said he and the boy were hunting for a Christmas tree when they saw a "greyish thing" gliding through the air making a strange noise at a very high rate of speed. He said it wasn't close enough for him to see its features, but it was huge and looked like nothing he had seen before.

Leport said the thing apparently came from the Ohio side of the river and for a while he thought it was going to land.

There have been many reports of a flying creature in the TNT area over the past several weeks. One theory is that it is a sand hill crane.

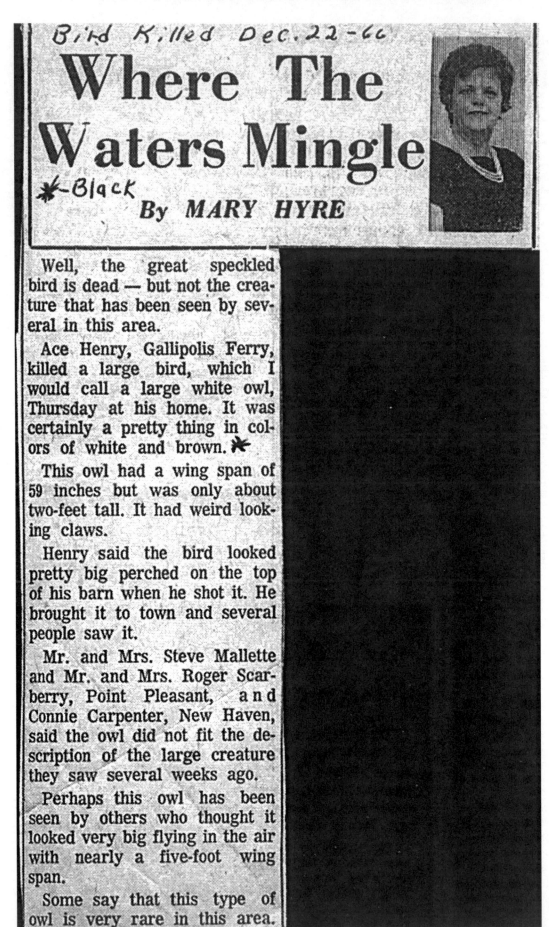

Bird Killed Dec. 22-66

Where The Waters Mingle

*-Black

By MARY HYRE

Well, the great speckled bird is dead — but not the creature that has been seen by several in this area.

Ace Henry, Gallipolis Ferry, killed a large bird, which I would call a large white owl, Thursday at his home. It was certainly a pretty thing in colors of white and brown. *

This owl had a wing span of 59 inches but was only about two-feet tall. It had weird looking claws.

Henry said the bird looked pretty big perched on the top of his barn when he shot it. He brought it to town and several people saw it.

Mr. and Mrs. Steve Mallette and Mr. and Mrs. Roger Scarberry, Point Pleasant, and Connie Carpenter, New Haven, said the owl did not fit the description of the large creature they saw several weeks ago.

Perhaps this owl has been seen by others who thought it looked very big flying in the air with nearly a five-foot wing span.

Some say that this type of owl is very rare in this area.

WVU Professor Says 'Bird' May Be Huge Crane

Everybody's getting into the act!

But the latest speculation on Mason County's famous "bird" comes from one who might know.

Dr. Robert Smith of the West Virginia University biology department told the Mason County Sheriff's Office this morning that the "bird" fits the description of a Sand Hill Crane.

He said the bird is native to the Midwest and also noted that it probably wouldn't stay in one place too long.

The crane described by Dr. Smith, who is sending a sketch, stands six or seven feet tall, has about an 80-inch wing span and has patches of red around its eyes. He said the eyes would be about six inches apart.

Dr. Smith said the crane would attack and possibly kill a dog but would not consume it. He also said the crane would attack people only if it becomes cornered or is wounded.

The professor talked to the Sheriff's Office about 10 minutes from Morgantown and said the University is interested in seeing the bird if it is killed or caught.

Deputy Millard Halstead said Dr. Smith told him he is interested in and is studying such birds.

Meanwhile, another possible sighting of the eyes of the bird was reported by Mary Hyre and a friend, who were scouting the TNT area where the creature was first seen Tuesday night.

Police said some 200 cars were in the area last night as citizens joined the search.

At the same time, reports of other people seeing the "bird" in recent months began to stream in.

One man would not identify himself because "people think those who see this thing are crazy."

He told The Register the "thing" appeared in his yard Tuesday night about 11:30. He said his dog started barking and the man went out and saw the bird rise and move southwesterly.

He said it was "cigar-shaped" and made a noise and "sounded like a Washington time signal. It seemed to have a motor or hum or move something like 15,000 to 18,000 rpm."

The man said his dog apparently was attacked. It had blood on it.

The bird was first sighted by two Point Pleasant couples Tuesday night.

A boy in Cheshire, O., also reported seeing the bird along Ohio Route 7.

Also, a Kanawha County gravedigger said he saw a "brown man" fly past him last week. Kenneth Duncan of Blue Creek near Charleston said he and some other men were digging his brother-in-law's grave on Saturday, when something that "looked like a brown human being" buzzed past.

"It was gliding through the trees and was in sight for about a minute," Duncan said. Four other men helping to dig the grave didn't see it.

Reports are still coming in but as yet the "bird" has not been captured. The incident is getting nationwide publicity.

WVU Professor Says 'Bird' May Be Huge Crane

Everybody's getting into the act!

But the latest speculation on Mason County's famous "bird" comes from one who might know.

Dr. Robert Smith of the West Virginia University biology department told the Mason County Sheriff's Office this morning that the "bird" fits the description of a Sand Hill Crane.

He said the bird is native to the Midwest and also noted that it probably wouldn't stay in one place too long.

The crane described by Dr. Smith, who is sending a sketch, stands six or seven feet tall, has about an 80-inch wing span and has patches of red around its eyes. He said the eyes would be about six inches apart.

Dr. Smith said the crane would attack and possibly kill a dog but would not consume it. He also said the crane would attack people only if it becomes cornered or is wounded.

The professor talked to the Sheriff's Office about 10 minutes from Morgantown and said the University is interested in seeing the bird if it is killed or caught.

Deputy Millard Halstead said Dr. Smith told him he is interested in and is studying such birds.

Meanwhile, another possible sighting of the eyes of the bird was reported by Mary Hyre and a friend, who were scouting the TNT area where the creature was first seen Tuesday night.

Police said some 200 cars were in the area last night as citizens joined the search.

At the same time, reports of other people seeing the "bird" in recent months began to stream in.

One man would not identify himself because "people think those who see this thing are crazy."

He told The Register the "thing" appeared in his yard Tuesday night about 11:30. He said his dog started barking and the man went out and saw the bird rise and move southwesterly.

He said it was "cigar-shaped" and made a noise and "sounded like a Washington time signal. It seemed to have a motor or hum or move something like 15,000 to 18,000 rpm."

The man said his dog apparently was attacked. It had blood on it.

The bird was first sighted by two Point Pleasant couples Tuesday night.

A boy in Cheshire, O., also reported seeing the bird along Ohio Route 7.

Also, a Kanawha County gravedigger said he saw a "brown man" fly past him last week. Kenneth Duncan of Blue Creek near Charleston said he and some other men were digging his brother-in-law's grave on Saturday, when something that "looked like a brown human being" buzzed past.

"It was gliding through the trees and was in sight for about a minute," Duncan said. Four other men helping to dig the grave didn't see it.

Reports are still coming in but as yet the "bird" has not been captured. The incident is getting nationwide publicity.

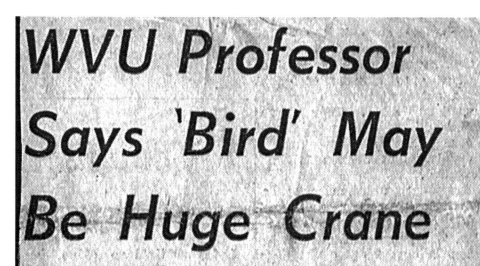

That Mothman: Would You Believe A Sandhill Crane?

That Mothman: Would You Believe A Sandhill Crane?

By RALPH TURNER

The case of the Mason County monster may have been solved Friday by a West Virginia University professor.

Dr. Robert L. Smith, associate professor of wildlife biology in WVU's division of forestry, told Mason Sheriff George Johnson at Point Pleasant he believes the "thing" which has been frightening people in the Point Pleasant area since Tuesday is a large bird which stopped off while migrating south.

"From all the descriptions I have read about this 'thing' it perfectly matches the sandhill crane," said the professor. "I definitely believe that's what these people are seeing."

Since Tuesday more than 10 people have spotted what they described as a "birdman" or "mothman" in the area of the McClintick Wildlife Station.

They described it as a huge gray-winged creature with large red eyes.

Dr. Smith said the sandhill crane stands an average of five feet and has gray plumage. A feature of its appearance is a bright red flesh area around each eye. It has an average wing spread of about seven feet.

"Somebody who had never seen anything like it before could easily get the impression it is a flying man," he said. "Car lights would cause the bare skin to reflect as big red circles around the eyes."

While such birds are rare to this area, Dr. Smith said this is migration time and it would not be too difficult for one or more of the birds to stop off at the wildlife refuge. There are no official sightings of such birds in West Virginia, although there have been unconfirmed reports in the past, he added.

The birds are rarely seen east of the Mississippi now except in Florida. Distribution mainly is in Canada and the population is increasing in the Midwest. They winter in Southern California, in Mexico and along the Gulf Coast.

According to one book, the sandhill crane is a "fit successor" to the great whooping crane which is almost extinct. The book states that the height of the male when it stands erect is nearly that of a man of average stature, while the bird's great wings carry its compact and muscular body with perfect ease at a high speed.

Dr. Smith said that while the birds are powerful fliers they cannot match the 100 m.p.h. speed one couple reported the "thing"

(See EERIE, Page 11)

Sandhill Crane: IFO (Identified Flying Object)?

The most popular theory about the Mothman was that it was just a misplaced sandhill crane—an endangered shore bird that stands six feet tall with a bright red patch of feathers on its head. Sandhill cranes, while extremely rare, are known to land near humans, strut, spread their wings, and draw their heads to their chest in a colorful display. However, none appear to have ever been documented flying at speeds over 100 miles per hour—their wings are built for soaring and gliding, not speed.

Firemen Make Latest Sighting

Eerie Cry Fits Description

(Continued From Page 1)

attained when pursuing their car.

Dr. Smith warned that while the sandhill crane is harmless if left alone, that if cornered it may become a formidable antagonist. Its dagger-like bill is a dangerous weapon which the crane does not hesitate to use when at bay and fighting for its life. Many a hunter's dog has been badly injured, he said.

Some of those who reported seeing the "monster" remembered best the eerie sound it made. The description of the sandhill crane also fits there.

"The cry of the sandhill crane is a veritable voice of nature, untamed and unterrified," says one book on birds. "Its uncanny quality is like that of the loon, but is more pronounced because of the much greater volume of the crane's voice. Its resonance is remarkable and its carrying power is increased by a distinct tremolo effect. Often for several minutes after the birds have vanished, the unearthly sound drifts back to the listener, like a taunting trumpet from the under-world."

Meanwhile, for the fourth night in a row, an area of the wildlife station again was clogged Friday night with the curious searching for the "thing".

The latest reported sighting came Friday morning from two Point Pleasant volunteer firemen, Captain Paul Yoder and Benjamin Enochs.

"As we were going into the picnic area in the TNT area, Paul and I saw this white shadow go across the car," Mr. Enochs reported. "This was about 1:30 a. m. Paul stopped the car and I went into the field, but couldn't see anything. I'd say this definitely was a large bird of some kind."

Meanwhile, authorities issued a warning to "monster hunters."

If the "thing" is a migratory crane they had better not shoot it. Migratory birds of all kinds are protected by federal and state wildlife laws.

Sheriff Johnson said he would arrest anybody caught with a loaded gun in the area after dark. There were earlier reports of armed people in the area.

Sheriff Johnson also warned that the scores of persons searching the abandoned powerhouse in the TNT area after dark risk possible serious injury.

'Moth-Man' Seen Crane

Point Pleasant Still Has Mystery

POINT PLEASANT (AP) —A big bird with a nasty disposition when aroused. That's the grus Mexicana, or more commonly called, the sandhill crane.

A West Virginia University scientist suggested Friday that the "moth-man" spotted by several people near this Ohio River city was this rare bird.

Robert Smith, associate professor of wildlife biology at WVU, told Mason County Sheriff George Johnson that the descriptions of eye-witnesses fit the huge sandhill crane, second largest of the crane family in America. Only the even rarer whopping crane is larger.

Smith noted that the sandhill crane is about as tall as a man when standing, and in flight its wings spread out to some six-and-a-half feet. It has a large bill, and it will use it to attack small animals or even human beings if molested.

The sandhill crane's breeding ground generally is considered the northern part of the U.S. and southern Canada, but it is seldom seen east of the Missis-

(Please turn to page two)

'MOTH-MAN' SEEN CRANE

(Continued from page one)

sippi river. The bird is migratory and winters in southern California, Mexico or along the Gulf Coast.

Smith said the behavior described by witnesses, following their automobiles, etc., has been observed in the sandhill crane.

Reference books say the large bird has been known to attack hunting dogs and wound or kill them with its long, sharp beak. Attacks on human beings also have been recorded.

Smith was of the opinion there has been no previous sightings of the large bird this far east. He said it may have followed migrating geese or other waterfowl to the McClintic Wildlife Station, a favored stopping place for migratory fowl, near here.

Source unknown

Not Mason Mothman, Is It An Owl?

POINT PLEASANT — Point Pleasant may well be tagged "Birdland" if bird stories and bird sightings continue to make news locally.

The newest story concerns another large, strange bird. However, this one is dead.

Ace Henry of Gallipolis Ferry, saw a large bird perched on his barn Tuesday night, and thinking it was a hawk shot it with a 20-gauge shotgun.

Henry reports the bird has a wingspan of about five feet and is two feet tall. The underside of the wings are white, and the rest is speckled with gray, with white rough around its eyes and white feathers covering its claws.

He said the bird is identical to a picture he has of a snowy owl. The snowy owl breeds in the Artic and migrates as far south as the Caribbean Sea.

Source unknown

Monster Returns To Mason

By MARY HYRE
Point Pleasant Correspondent

POINT PLEASANT — Six — or maybe seven — more people became believers in the Mason County Monster Wednesday night.

What is it they saw? They don't know, but they have managed to convince a raft of people they saw something.

The latest observers of the red-eyed, wing-backed six-foot thing are Mr. and Mrs. Raymond Wamsley; Ricky, Connie and Vickie Thomas and Marcella Bennett.

They spotted the monster around 9 p. m. Wednesday outside the home of Mr. and Mrs. Ralph Thomas, in the TNT area, where the thing was sighted Tuesday night.

Observer number seven is reported to be a Cheshire area youth who allegedly was chased by a thing matching the description of the Mason County Monster. The chase took place on Route 7 in Ohio.

Wednesday night's sighting took place as the Wamsley's and the Thomas children were leaving the Thomas home. They said the red-eyed creature was lying on the road behind a car.

Giant Owl Killed On Area Farm

Bird Killed 12-22-66

A bird although a dead one, is in the news again and the big question is — Is it or isn't it one that may have been spotted here on several occasions?

Apparently from the discription it is not the one that was seen by two young couples last month, but may be one that has kept cropping into headlines since that time.

A large owl uncommon to this area, was killed Tuesday night by Ace Henry on his farm at Gallipolis Ferry.

The bird, which has a wing spread of nearly five feet, has several areas of white and is speckled with black. On the under side of the wings the plumage is snowy white, and white fur-like feathers encircle the large eyes and cover the claws.

Henry said he shot it with a 20-gauge shotgun Tuesday night after it was spotted sitting on top of his barn. He said at first he thought it was a hawk but after killing it he was perplexed to know its true identity.

The Register Editorial staff, in an attempt to identify the bird, has concluded that it is a snowy owl.

The snowy owl is an inhabitant of northern regions, where his coloring blends with the snowy surroundings. In the winter it travels south through the states and sometimes as far as Texas. On the wing it is so swift that it will overtake a grouse in flight.

This killing of this owl is mentioned by Linda Scarberry in her interview in Chapter 3.

FANTASY OR FACT—Residents of Mason County who have been chasing a strange manlike flying thing—whether it be-a-monster or behemoth—now have something tangilble to look at. Jack Park, Point Pleasant, has painted a large fierce bird based on various descriptions of the thing which has been spotted several times in Northern West Virginia since Nov. 17. Deputy Sheriff Millard Halstead photographed the artists' conception in the TNT area, near Point Pleasant where the thing was spotted numerous times. Officials report the isolated area is still packed each night with car loads of people searching for the monster.

Page 30 — THE MESSENGER, Athens, Ohio — Sunday, Jan. 22, 1967

Where The Waters Mingle

By MARY HYRE

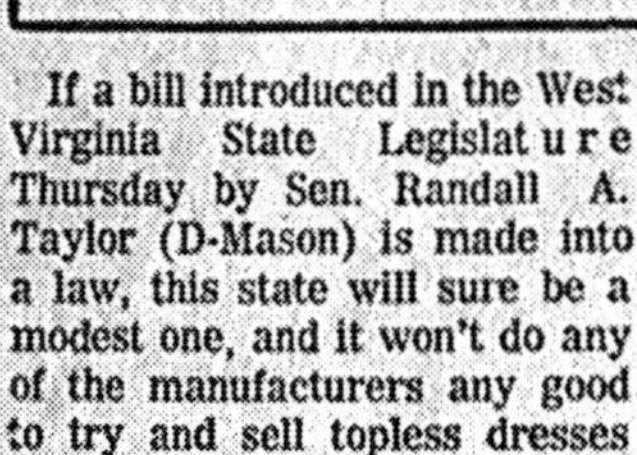

If a bill introduced in the West Virginia State Legislature Thursday by Sen. Randall A. Taylor (D-Mason) is made into a law, this state will sure be a modest one, and it won't do any of the manufacturers any good to try and sell topless dresses or bathing suits in this state.

Senator Taylor introduced a "nudist" bill which would make it unlawful to undress in the presence of others, so if you go to take a bath, be sure you don't forget the soap or towel before you undress and jump in the bathtub, because you can not call for help if this law goes into effect.

One lady told me she was quite concerned about the bill because of the poor little children who would not be able to have a bath until they are old enough to undress and bathe themselves, since the bill says it will be unlawful to undress in front of others.

One man told me that he was wondering just how the evidence is going to be sought to see if a man and wife undress dence is going to be sought to see if a man and wife undress in the same room. He said there sure are going to have to be a lot of Peeping Toms.

It was also brought to my attention that perhaps the doctors should fight this bill, because they wouldn't be able to have the nurses undress the patients in preparing for examinations, and the people would all have to go to another state to see a doctor. I bet the nurses will be happy that they will no longer have to give patients a bath. If they do, it will sure have to be under cover.

Another measure will have to be taken at the swimming pools, because the state law requires one to take a shower before entering the pool, so there will be a big line waiting at the shower stalls. Also, the athletic boys will all have to be very modest and have private shower rooms.

What about the boy who wants to take off for his favorite swimming hole or the river and swim in the nude? That would also be a thing of the past.

I feel that if this becomes a law, it will be one that is violated more than any law ever made. What do you think?

Senator Taylor offered the bill in the Senate to fight nudist camps in the state, and since Mason County has one, he would like to make it a law that it is a misdemeanor to sell land for such purposes.

It seems that West Virginia is seeing its share of strange objects. The latest was by Tad Jones of Dunbar who said he came upon the Unidentified Flying Object on Interstate 64. Its description is like that of many which have been reported in many areas of the United States and around the world.

One woman in Point Pleasant reported several weeks ago about seeing something like that but it was in the air several hundred feet. There are also, of course, the sightings of the monster and the unidentified objects seen recently by people in Cheshire, Gallipolis, Eureka and Addison.

There is an interesting article in the February issue of True Magazine by John Keel of New York, who was here doing research for another article about the strange sightings in this area. The latter article will probably appear in the August or September issue.

In the article appearing this month, he says that each new sighting only adds to the mystery, one that the government has assigned scientists at the University of Colorado to solve. Any immediate solution how- University of Colorado to solve. Any immediate solution, how-ever, seems improable.

The origins and motovations of these creatures, if they are real, can only be speculated. But millions of people throughout the world are now convinced that something is going on, and that there is "somebody out there." More and more, respected scientists are beginning to take the matter seriously as they delve into the question of life on other worlds.

Gigantic, Fuzzy Bird Chases Auto In Storm

POINT PLEASANT — The "monster," which created perhaps one of the most bizarre surprise incidents in Mason County last December, was seen again last week during a heavy rain storm by a Middleport resident who asked that his name not be published.

The man said that the large fuzzy thing started hovering over his car near New Haven on Route 33 and followed him to the golf course just north of Mason.

He said its wing span was as wide as the highway and its fuzzy wings hung down on each side of the car. He said it frightended him very much, although he could see nothing but the wings.

Last December four Point Pleasant people, Mr. and Mrs. Roger Scarberry and Mr. and Mrs. Steve Mallette, were chased by a strange bird-like object from the TNT area to the city limits. They said it had a wide wing span and red eyes. Others also saw it later when it chased their cars.

Sunday night a couple reported that while traveling on Route 17 for several miles toward Point Pleasant, a bright light went across the highway in front of them in a ball shape and then followed them on the hill side to Henderson. Then it sent in a southern direction and disappeared. Many other similar sightings have also been reported.

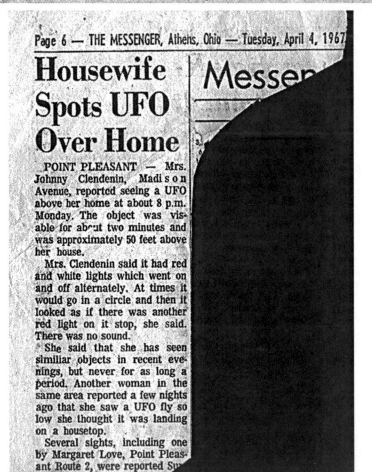

Page 6 — THE MESSENGER, Athens, Ohio — Tuesday, April 4, 1967

Housewife Spots UFO Over Home

POINT PLEASANT — Mrs. Johnny Clendenin, Madison Avenue, reported seeing a UFO above her home at about 8 p.m. Monday. The object was visable for about two minutes and was approximately 50 feet above her house.

Mrs. Clendenin said it had red and white lights which went on and off alternately. At times it would go in a circle and then it looked as if there was another red light on it stop, she said. There was no sound.

She said that she has seen similiar objects in recent evenings, but never for as long a period. Another woman in the same area reported a few nights ago that she saw a UFO fly so low she thought it was landing on a housetop.

Several sights, including one by Margaret Love, Point Pleasant Route 2, were reported Sunday night.

Messen

Youths Spot UFO In Sky Over Point

POINT PLEASANT — Two 14-year-old Cleveland youths will remember their Easter vacation in Point Pleasant for a long time. Monday night the young visitors reported seeing an unidentified object in the sky over 39th Street.

Keith Scarberry and Justin Clark said that at 10 p.m. they saw a white object with a tail in the sky. They said they were paralyzed with fright for a few seconds before the object suddenly disappeared.

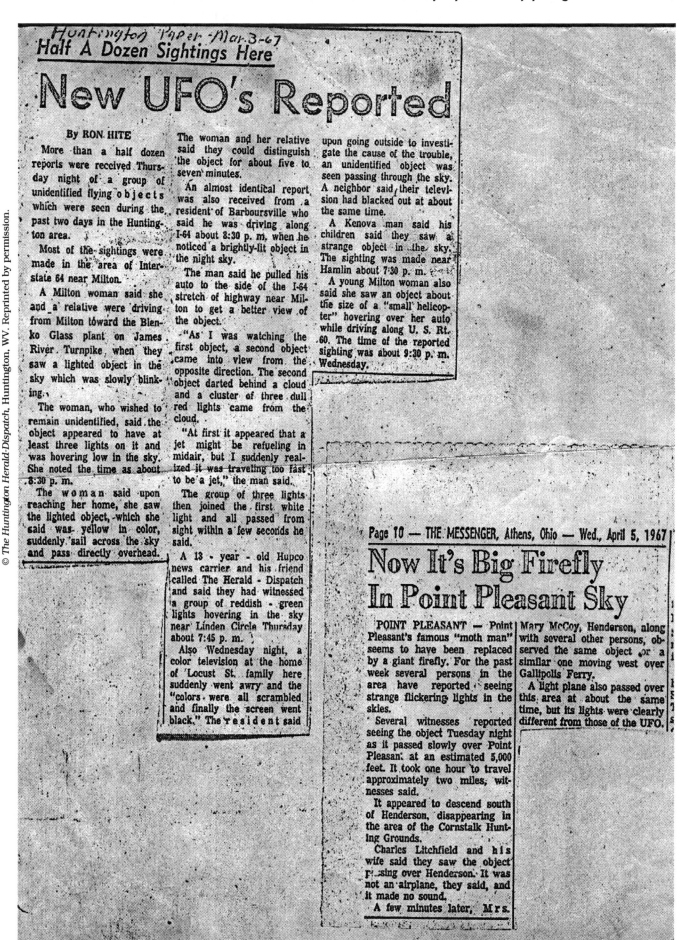

Huntington Paper - Mar. 3-67

Half A Dozen Sightings Here

New UFO's Reported

By RON HITE

More than a half dozen reports were received Thursday night of a group of unidentified flying objects which were seen during the past two days in the Huntington area.

Most of the sightings were made in the area of Interstate 64 near Milton.

A Milton woman said she and a relative were driving from Milton toward the Blenko Glass plant on James River Turnpike when they saw a lighted object in the sky which was slowly blinking.

The woman, who wished to remain unidentified, said the object appeared to have at least three lights on it and was hovering low in the sky. She noted the time as about 8:30 p. m.

The woman said upon reaching her home, she saw the lighted object, which she said was yellow in color, suddenly sail across the sky and pass directly overhead.

The woman and her relative said they could distinguish the object for about five to seven minutes.

An almost identical report was also received from a resident of Barboursville who said he was driving along I-64 about 8:30 p. m. when he noticed a brightly-lit object in the night sky.

The man said he pulled his auto to the side of the I-64 stretch of highway near Milton to get a better view of the object.

"As I was watching the first object, a second object came into view from the opposite direction. The second object darted behind a cloud and a cluster of three dull red lights came from the cloud.

"At first it appeared that a jet might be refueling in midair, but I suddenly realized it was traveling too fast to be a jet," the man said.

The group of three lights then joined the first white light and all passed from sight within a few seconds he said.

A 13 - year - old Hupco news carrier and his friend called The Herald - Dispatch and said they had witnessed a group of reddish - green lights hovering in the sky near Linden Circle Thursday about 7:45 p. m.

Also Wednesday night, a color television at the home of Locust St. family here suddenly went awry and the "colors were all scrambled and finally the screen went black." The resident said upon going outside to investigate the cause of the trouble, an unidentified object was seen passing through the sky. A neighbor said their television had blacked out at about the same time.

A Kenova man said his children said they saw a strange object in the sky. The sighting was made near Hamlin about 7:30 p. m.

A young Milton woman also said she saw an object about the size of a "small helicopter" hovering over her auto while driving along U. S. Rt. 60. The time of the reported sighting was about 9:30 p. m. Wednesday.

Page 10 — THE MESSENGER, Athens, Ohio — Wed., April 5, 1967

Now It's Big Firefly In Point Pleasant Sky

POINT PLEASANT — Point Pleasant's famous "moth man" seems to have been replaced by a giant firefly. For the past week several persons in the area have reported seeing strange flickering lights in the skies.

Several witnesses reported seeing the object Tuesday night as it passed slowly over Point Pleasant at an estimated 5,000 feet. It took one hour to travel approximately two miles, witnesses said.

It appeared to descend south of Henderson, disappearing in the area of the Cornstalk Hunting Grounds.

Charles Litchfield and his wife said they saw the object passing over Henderson. It was not an airplane, they said, and it made no sound.

A few minutes later, Mrs. Mary McCoy, Henderson, along with several other persons, observed the same object or a similar one moving west over Gallipolis Ferry.

A light plane also passed over this area at about the same time, but its lights were clearly different from those of the UFO.

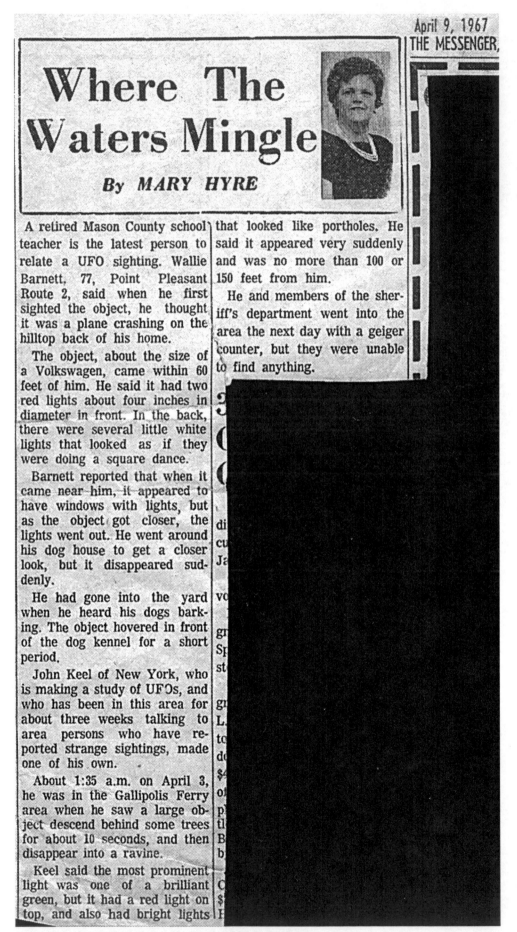

April 9, 1967
THE MESSENGER,

Where The Waters Mingle

By MARY HYRE

A retired Mason County school teacher is the latest person to relate a UFO sighting. Wallie Barnett, 77, Point Pleasant Route 2, said when he first sighted the object, he thought it was a plane crashing on the hilltop back of his home.

The object, about the size of a Volkswagen, came within 60 feet of him. He said it had two red lights about four inches in diameter in front. In the back, there were several little white lights that looked as if they were doing a square dance.

Barnett reported that when it came near him, it appeared to have windows with lights, but as the object got closer, the lights went out. He went around his dog house to get a closer look, but it disappeared suddenly.

He had gone into the yard when he heard his dogs barking. The object hovered in front of the dog kennel for a short period.

John Keel of New York, who is making a study of UFOs, and who has been in this area for about three weeks talking to area persons who have reported strange sightings, made one of his own.

About 1:35 a.m. on April 3, he was in the Gallipolis Ferry area when he saw a large object descend behind some trees for about 10 seconds, and then disappear into a ravine.

Keel said the most prominent light was one of a brilliant green, but it had a red light on top, and also had bright lights that looked like portholes. He said it appeared very suddenly and was no more than 100 or 150 feet from him.

He and members of the sheriff's department went into the area the next day with a geiger counter, but they were unable to find anything.

Page 18 — THE MESSENGER, Athens, Ohio — Thurs., April 13, 1967

UFO's Sighted Again At Camp Conley, Mason

POINT PLEASANT — The UFO's have been sighted nightly again in many parts of Mason County.

The James Lilly family at Camp Conley have seen as many as six in one night for nearly three weeks.

The Lillys report many people come and watch with them. The objects appear in many different directions, but apparently come from the TNT area. The sightings sometimes are very close. Objects are red and white and sometimes travel very fast while other times go very slow, without sound. Witnesses agree the objects aren't airplanes.

One UFO came very close to the Lilly home, illuminating the house. Their television went on the blink for a short time.

Mrs. Lilly and children Linda and Garry said a 'big bright" object followed them from Route 62 to their home one night. Their daughter-in-law, Doris Lilly, has also seen these objects. Johnny Lilly said that one night it looked as if an object had diamond-shaped windows in it.

The Lillys say that they do not know what it is, but there sure is something.

It was also reported that in the Mason area two bright red lights hovered over that area Tuesday night.

More than a dozen people saw the UFO Wednesday night at the Lilly home.

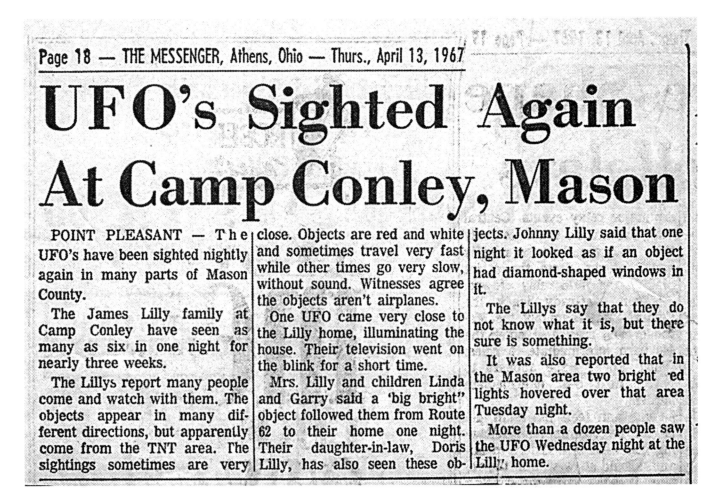

At right is one of the first clippings announcing the arrival of John Keel, author of "The Mothman Prophecies." Mr. Keel was a guest at the home of Linda Scarberry and her parents while conducting research for his book.

UFO Writer Coming Here; Sighting Told

John Keel, free-lance writer from New York who has been spending numerous months digging into UFO reports, will be in Point Pleasant the next two weeks doing research.

He will be available to lecture to any group interested.

Keel was here several months ago when the "bird" was cited, writing for True magazine.

He is a well-known writer and is fast becoming a top "ufologist" in the nation.

Meanwhile, there were reports that as many as 20 people in downtown Point Pleasant sighted an unidentified flying

Object Seen Near Cha rleston

Dunbar Man Alleges He Examined UFO

CHARLESTON — An appliance store owner at nearby Dunbar reported that he stood within 10 feet of an unidentified flying object and described it as "completely round like a ball."

Tad Jones said he drove up to the strange object on Interstate 64, about six miles from downtown Charleston in midmorning.

"I sighted this object quite a distance from the road and thought it must be state road commission equipment," Jones said. "I couldn't drive around it because it was about 20 feet in diameter and blocked the westbound driving lanes.

"I got out of my truck, walked up and looked it over," Jones said. "It was hovering above the roadway about three or four feet. It had four wheels and in the bottom of the ball was a propeller-like apparatus which was revolving noiselessly.

"At the top was a round window with two antennae," Jones continued. "In the middle of the object was a protruding flange, or seam, which indicated to me that it had been connected together in some way. It was aluminum in color. I looked up at the window but didn't see anyone.

"I stood there a minute and then it gently rose and—without any exhaust, any odor or any noise whatsoever, it went straight up. I watched it for what must have been a minute or a minute and-a-half until it passed from sight.

"I was amazed. It was sometime before I got back in the truck and went on to work, and quite a bit later before I decided I had better report this to the Guthrie,, W. Va. Air Force Base radar force."

A spokesman at the Guthrie base said radar operators had not detected any unusual object on their radar screens at the time of the reported sighting but that the matter " was being investigated for transmission to higher headquarters."

Students Find

Five Day Forecast

Temperatures Saturday through Wednesday will average above normal with daily highs ranging from the upper 30s to the upper 40s while nighttime lows will be in the middle 20s and lower 30s.

Warming most of period but change to colder by middle of next week.

Athens Messenger

April 23, 1967

TNT Area Again Scene Of Sighting

POINT PLEASANT — A traffic cop will be needed in the Camp Conley area if UFOs continue to pass over that area. It was reported that last night the area was packed full of cars. Th TNT aeea is also a site where hundreds of people are going nightly to look for UFOs.

One was seen again last night. A unidentified plane was nearby and as it started toward the area ground observers said the UFO disappeared.

.he TNT area last night looked like the traffic flow when the "monster" was seen in that area last November.

Page 16 — THE MESSENGER, Athens, Ohio — Friday, April 21, 1967

UFO Mystery Solved? Many Say No

POINT PLEASANT — Three Mason County Civil Defense unit members say they have solved the mysterious UFO sightings reported in the Point Pleasant area in recent weeks, but their claim is disputed by many area residents.

The three, Richard Newell, Carl Sibley and Lou Mueller concluded that the sightings had resulted from lights on the front, wings and rear of a commercial airliner. The trio took a plane flight around the area Thursday night.

They point out that Allegheny Airlines flight 823 makes daily trips into Huntington from eastern cities and a return flight in the evening, noting that sightings were made between 8:10 and 8:50 p.m.

Those who dispute the claim say that the trio's explanation might cover some of the sightings, but they are quick to point out that sightings have also been made later in the evening — around midnight. The question has also been raised about the likelihood of a plane coming right at a car in the manner that the strang lights have been reported.

Recent reports have also indicated that objects have been sighted in formations, with as many as five to eight objects at one time.

News Briefs

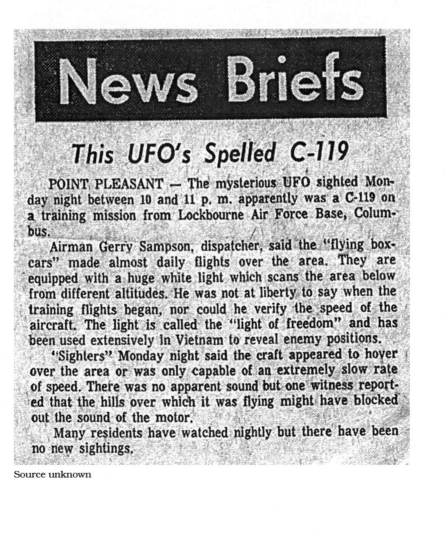

This UFO's Spelled C-119

POINT PLEASANT — The mysterious UFO sighted Monday night between 10 and 11 p. m. apparently was a C-119 on a training mission from Lockbourne Air Force Base, Columbus.

Airman Gerry Sampson, dispatcher, said the "flying boxcars" made almost daily flights over the area. They are equipped with a huge white light which scans the area below from different altitudes. He was not at liberty to say when the training flights began, nor could he verify the speed of the aircraft. The light is called the "light of freedom" and has been used extensively in Vietnam to reveal enemy positions.

"Sighters" Monday night said the craft appeared to hover over the area or was only capable of an extremely slow rate of speed. There was no apparent sound but one witness reported that the hills over which it was flying might have blocked out the sound of the motor.

Many residents have watched nightly but there have been no new sightings.

Source unknown

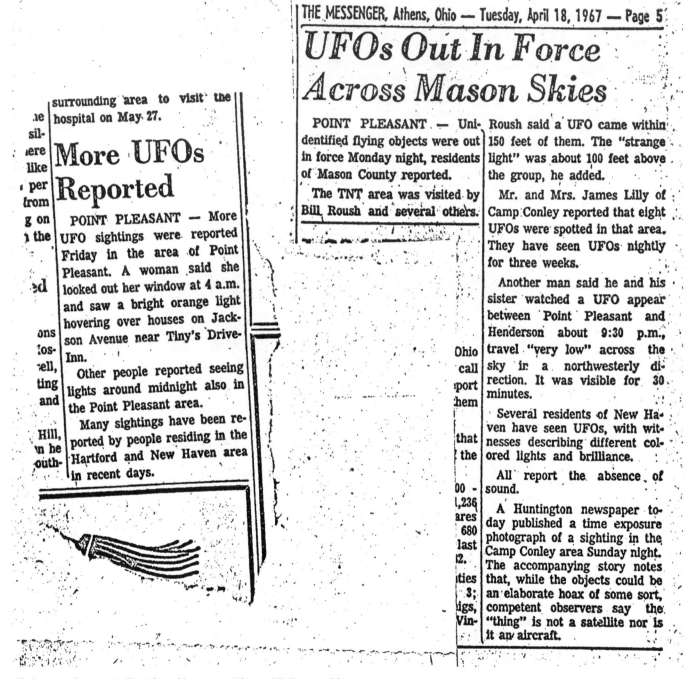

surrounding area to visit the hospital on May 27.

More UFOs Reported

POINT PLEASANT — More UFO sightings were reported Friday in the area of Point Pleasant. A woman said she looked out her window at 4 a.m. and saw a bright orange light hovering over houses on Jackson Avenue near Tiny's Drive-Inn.

Other people reported seeing lights around midnight also in the Point Pleasant area.

Many sightings have been reported by people residing in the Hartford and New Haven area in recent days.

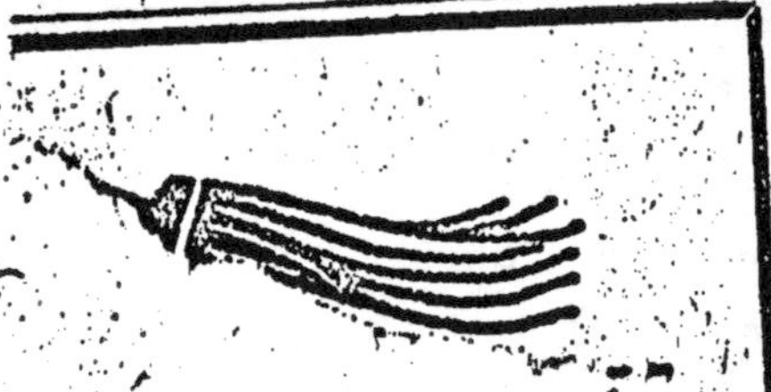

THE MESSENGER, Athens, Ohio — Tuesday, April 18, 1967 — Page 5

UFOs Out In Force Across Mason Skies

POINT PLEASANT — Unidentified flying objects were out in force Monday night, residents of Mason County reported.

The TNT area was visited by Bill Roush and several others.

Roush said a UFO came within 150 feet of them. The "strange light" was about 100 feet above the group, he added.

Mr. and Mrs. James Lilly of Camp Conley reported that eight UFOs were spotted in that area. They have seen UFOs nightly for three weeks.

Another man said he and his sister watched a UFO appear between Point Pleasant and Henderson about 9:30 p.m., travel "very low" across the sky in a northwesterly direction. It was visible for 30 minutes.

Several residents of New Haven have seen UFOs, with witnesses describing different colored lights and brilliance.

All report the absence of sound.

A Huntington newspaper today published a time exposure photograph of a sighting in the Camp Conley area Sunday night. The accompanying story notes that, while the objects could be an elaborate hoax of some sort, competent observers say the "thing" is not a satellite nor is it an aircraft.

UFO Watching Picks Up; Object Outruns Pilot

By CELIA AEIKER
Register Staff Writer

Apparently the newest fad in the Point Pleasant area is UFO watching, unidentified flying objects have been visiting the night skies for well over three weeks now and scores of persons have been reporting sightings.

Tuesday night a Gallipolis-based airplane whose pilot prefers to remain anonymous reportedly pursued a light - bearing object over the area at 2,400 feet. The object was rapidly moving in a northerly direction when spotted.

The pilot said he flashed the landing lights on his own aircraft as he closed in but the object disappeared before he and a companion could determine its shape and size..

Observers on the ground said the UFO, which bore red and white lights, passed overhead at around 8:05 p.m.

A similar object has been observed along Route 62, in the area of the Pleasant Point Resort, almost nightly, usually between 7 and 9 p.m. In the past few days the area has been lined with cars and spectators hoping for a glimpse of the mysterious object.

A number of persons in the TNT area Monday night, including Bill Roush and several others, reported that UFO came within 150 feet of them. Mr. Roush said the "strange light" was about 100 feet above the group.

Mr. and Mrs. James Lilly of Camp Conley, the scene of many sightings, reported that eight UFOs were spotted in that area the same night.

Still another man and his sister said they watched a UFO traveling in a northwesterly direction between Point Pleasant and Henderson. The sighting took place around 9:30 p.m. Monday.

A Huntington newspaper Tuesday published a time exposure photograph taken of an object which was sighted in the Camp Conley area Sunday night. The article stated that while the objects could be an elaborate hoax of some sort competent observers say the thing is not a satellite or airplane.

Residents from New Haven and other parts of the county also have reported sighting objects with lights of varying degrees of brilliancy.

Monday night the Meigs County Sheriff's Department received telephone calls from where residents reported seeing an unidentified flying object. Observers said the object resembled a silver disc, was lighted by revolving lights and was flying low and at tremendous speed.

The TNT area was again filled with cars and people Wednesday night on the alert for UFOs. Deputy Millard Halstead and others sighted an object with red and white lights near the Hidden Valley Country Club around 8:30 last night. The object passed slowly overhead, appearing to glide, Halstead said.

Civil Defense Director Andy Wilson and other Civil Defende personnel have also reported seeing the objects and could offer no explanation for them.

Whatever the objects are, they are the talk of the town. Many people have taken to holding watch parties and all -night vigils in hopes of getting a look at the aerial phenomena which, it would appear, has made its home in Point Pleasant for the time being.

Saucer Hunting Is New Warm Weather Sport

POINT PLEASANT — Warm weather has aided the "saucer hunting" craze which has swept the area.

Friday night, the TNT and Camp Conley area was filled

with people looking for the UFO's which have been spotted by several people lately.

These unidentified flying objects have been seen in the area for over three weeks and as many as eight sightings have been reported in one night. Friday night several people reported a sighting over 30th Street.

The objects vary in color. Some are just one red light, while others change from red to white and sometimes throw in a little blue and green.

Friday night one observer watched them through a telescope and said that they were definitely not planes, but round objects.

As with last year's "flying monster," the public is baffled as to just what they really are.

Still More UFO's Seen In Point Pleasant Sky

POINT PLEASANT — Unidentified flying objects were spotted over Point Pleasant again Thursday night.

At about 7:40 p. m., Mr. and Mrs. Scotty Soladean, Henderson, and others who saw the object Wednesday night reported seeing a bright light go over Point Pleasant again. It made no sound, they said.

Soladean said that fire appeared to fall from the object just before it disappeared Wednesday night. He said that if was a strange looking light and that it hung very still in the sky. If it had been an airplane he could have heard it, he said.

J. A. (Andy) Wilson, director of Civil Defense; George Carson, also working with Civil Defense; Robert Spears, Mount Vernon Ave., of the National Guard, and Don Nott said that they saw the UFO from the top of the courthouse at about 10 p. m. They said it had a bright light and that it came from the direction of the Methodist Church.

Charles Fry, also with the National Guard, and numerous others reported seeing the UFO Thursday night.

Several UFO's Spotted Over Holiday Weekend

POINT PLEASANT — The UFO's were out in many areas Monday night as theey have been for several nights.

Monday night at 10 p.m. a bright light rose from a low position in the north section of Point Pleasant, then made a circle southeast. Then it met with another UFO that made the same circle as the first one, only in the opposite direction. At times the big light would be very bright, then it would fade away and at times go completely out all at once.

In the Mason area it was reported that people said this red object looked like a big ball of fire and that it turned to a white light that was also bright before it disappeared.

In Hartford, residents say that for several nights similar objects have been very low in that area.

In other areas people have seen these strange lights and reported that their cars would almost stall and the lights get very dim on the car while the object was near.

It's Saucers On Parade . . .

Reports apparently confirming recent sightings of unidentified flying objects in the Tri-State Area continued to mount Friday.

Scores of persons have now said they have seen strange objects in the sky which defy description except in the "flying saucer" category.

Another UFO

An unidentified flying object with brilliant white lights which later changed to red over Huntington was sighted about 9 p. m. Thursday. One observer telephoned Tri-State Airport and was told there were no aircraft in the area.

UFO Seen Here Late Wednesday

An unidentified flying object passed over downtown Point Pleasant late Wednesday evening, witnesses reported, and tied up traffic in the Sixth Street area as motorists stopped their cars to watch.

The UFO was sighted by a number of persons including around 30 people leaving the Church of Christ in Christian Union following a service.

One witness said the object glowed brightly and appeared to be circular in shape. It was last seen heading past Central School.

Wed., May 10, 1967 — Page 19

Bright UFO Resembles Stove Pipe

POINT PLEASANT — UFO sightings were reported in several areas again last night with one of the brightest lights ever witnessed.

There were two in most areas where it was reported to be. One was very bright and very large. Some reported that it looked as if it had an object resembling a stove pipe at the top. The other UFO was bright orange encircled in black.

Both traveled northwest and was seen between 9 p.m. and 3 a.m.

DANCE SATURDAY

POMEROY — Pomeroy High School will sponsor a high school

Unusual Objects In Sky Spotted In Three Counties

POINT PLEASANT —UFO's have made quite a display since Sunday night in three counties, Mason, Putnam and Roane.

Sunday night just before dark a long, black object with no wings or any visable gear glided very low over Point Pleasant.

A few hours later north of Point Pleasant, several people saw a white light very low in the east. Among the people seeing the bright light was John A. Keel, a noted Ufologist, writer and lecturer. Keel has done extensive research on UFO sightings and has traveled many miles during the past year.

The white light was visable for about ten minutes, bobbed up and down and suddenly vanished.

A Putnam County man, Albert Brown, a shift superintendent at the new mining operations at Elmwood, reported that when he left work at 12:45 Monday morning he noticed a strange white light very low as he traveled toward his Buffalo home. On Tribble Road and Route 35, this oject stayed in his view.

He said he finally stopped and watched the UFO, and it turned colors of blue and orange and bobbed up and down. It would first be on top of the hill, then disappear behind the hill and then reappear. He tried to find a road that would lead him to where it seemed to be stationary, but was unable to do so.

He noted that he parked his truck and watched the object for about four hours and then went home and awakened his wife, Shirley, to show her what he had seen. She reported that it was the brightest and strangest light she had ever seen.

Brown, deciding that this was something that should be investigated, called the Civil Defense in Charleston. But they told him to call the state police. The object had gone by the time they arrived.

Mrs. Brown said she had received a call from Gary Davison, Spencer, who said he had seen a similar object in the Spencer area Sunday evening about 7 p.m.

Meetings In Meigs

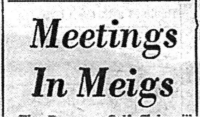

FIVE UFO'S SEEN IN MASON

POINT PLEASANT — A cluster of five disc-shaped, aluminum-colored objects were sighted in the TNT area of Mason County late Thursday afternoon.

Reporting this latest in a long series of UFO sightings in Mason and Meigs counties were Mr. and Mrs. Ronald Plantz, 35 Burdette Addition. Three other persons also saw the objects.

The objects were seen near the old powerhouse in the area where the so-called "Mason County Monster" was first spotted by four Point Pleasant youth last November. That monster, most often described as a huge bird with a tremendous wingspan and fiery eyes, apparently has left the area after being repeatedly seen for a number of weeks.

In the latest UFO sighting, the Plantzs reported that the five objects, in a cluster formation, circled about 400 feet in the air.

They came out of the cluster formation and formed a straight line, heading northward about one mile apart, then circled and went across the Ohio River and out of sight. The objects were in sight for approximately 15 minutes.

Witnesses said there were two red lights, one a bright red circular type and the other stationary. They said the objects sometimes were so near the ground that trees obscured the view. There was no detectable sound. All the witnesses agreed that the objects, whatever they might have been, definitely were not airplanes.

Meanwhile, three Mason County Civil Defense workers assert they have "solved" some of the recent sightings in the Point Pleasant area. After taking a flight over the area Thursday night, the men concluded that the sightings resulted from lights on the front, wings and rear of a commercial airliner. Richard Newell, Carl Sibley and Lou Nueller said an Allegheny Airlines plane goes over the area between 8:10 and 8:50 p.m. nightly.

However, their conclusions immediately were challenged by persons who have reported seeing UFOs. These believers said that they were aware of commercial flights in the area, but that the UFOs were soundless and occurred at different times. UFOs also are disc-shaped instead of having the configurations of airplanes.

So the mystery, now six months old, continues without a plausible explanation.

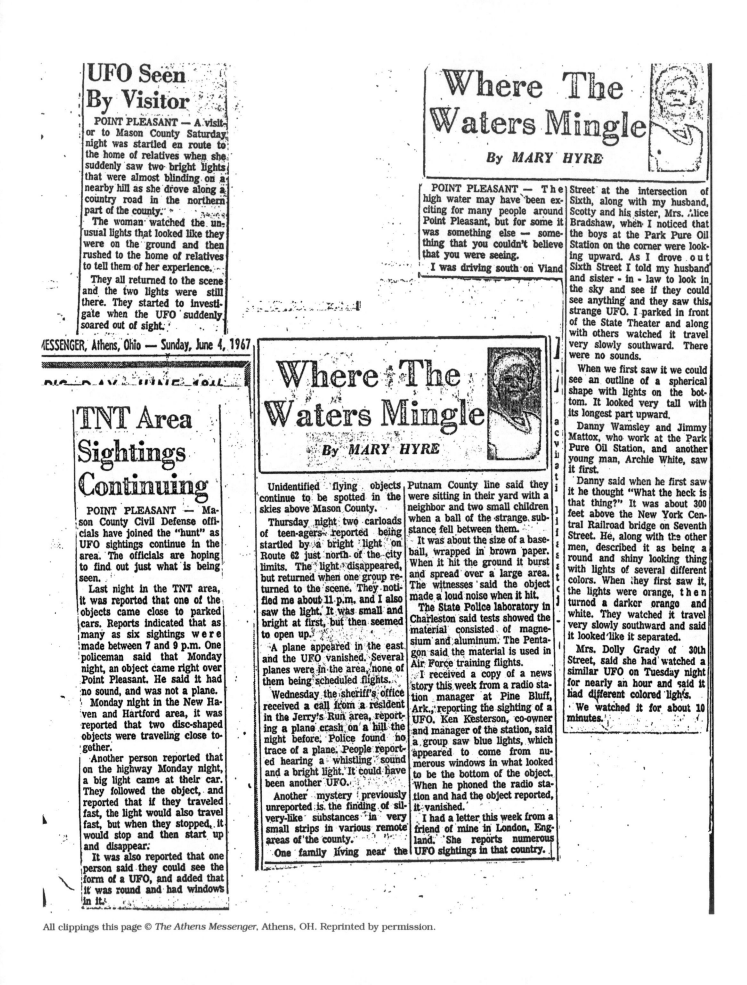

UFO Seen By Visitor

POINT PLEASANT — A visitor to Mason County Saturday night was startled en route to the home of relatives when she suddenly saw two bright lights that were almost blinding on a nearby hill as she drove along a country road in the northern part of the county.

The woman watched the unusual lights that looked like they were on the ground and then rushed to the home of relatives to tell them of her experience.

They all returned to the scene and the two lights were still there. They started to investigate when the UFO suddenly soared out of sight.

MESSENGER, Athens, Ohio — Sunday, June 4, 1967

TNT Area Sightings Continuing

POINT PLEASANT — Mason County Civil Defense officials have joined the "hunt" as UFO sightings continue in the area. The officials are hoping to find out just what is being seen.

Last night in the TNT area, it was reported that one of the objects came close to parked cars. Reports indicated that as many as six sightings were made between 7 and 9 p.m. One policeman said that Monday night, an object came right over Point Pleasant. He said it had no sound, and was not a plane.

Monday night in the New Haven and Hartford area, it was reported that two disc-shaped objects were traveling close together.

Another person reported that on the highway Monday night, a big light came at their car. They followed the object, and reported that if they traveled fast, the light would also travel fast, but when they stopped, it would stop and then start up and disappear.

It was also reported that one person said they could see the form of a UFO, and added that it was round and had windows in it.

Where The Waters Mingle

By MARY HYRE

Unidentified flying objects continue to be spotted in the skies above Mason County.

Thursday night two carloads of teen-agers reported being startled by a bright light on Route 62 just north of the city limits. The light disappeared, but returned when one group returned to the scene. They notified me about 11 p.m. and I also saw the light. It was small and bright at first, but then seemed to open up.

A plane appeared in the east and the UFO vanished. Several planes were in the area, none of them being scheduled flights.

Wednesday the sheriff's office received a call from a resident in the Jerry's Run area, reporting a plane crash on a hill the night before. Police found no trace of a plane. People reported hearing a whistling sound and a bright light. It could have been another UFO.

Another mystery previously unreported is the finding of silvery-like substances in very small strips in various remote areas of the county.

One family living near the Putnam County line said they were sitting in their yard with a neighbor and two small children when a ball of the strange substance fell between them.

It was about the size of a baseball, wrapped in brown paper. When it hit the ground it burst and spread over a large area. The witnesses said the object made a loud noise when it hit.

The State Police laboratory in Charleston said tests showed the material consisted of magnesium and aluminum. The Pentagon said the material is used in Air Force training flights.

I received a copy of a news story this week from a radio station manager at Pine Bluff, Ark., reporting the sighting of a UFO. Ken Kesterson, co-owner and manager of the station, said a group saw blue lights, which appeared to come from numerous windows in what looked to be the bottom of the object. When he phoned the radio station and had the object reported, it vanished.

I had a letter this week from a friend of mine in London, England. She reports numerous UFO sightings in that country.

Where The Waters Mingle

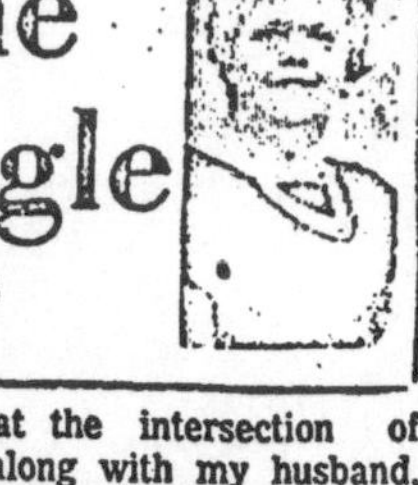

By MARY HYRE

POINT PLEASANT — The high water may have been exciting for many people around Point Pleasant, but for some it was something else — something that you couldn't believe that you were seeing.

I was driving south on Viand Street at the intersection of Sixth, along with my husband, Scotty and his sister, Mrs. Alice Bradshaw, when I noticed that the boys at the Park Pure Oil Station on the corner were looking upward. As I drove out Sixth Street I told my husband and sister - in - law to look in the sky and see if they could see anything and they saw this strange UFO. I parked in front of the State Theater and along with others watched it travel very slowly southward. There were no sounds.

When we first saw it we could see an outline of a spherical shape with lights on the bottom. It looked very tall with its longest part upward.

Danny Wamsley and Jimmy Mattox, who work at the Park Pure Oil Station, and another young man, Archie White, saw it first.

Danny said when he first saw it he thought "What the heck is that thing?" It was about 300 feet above the New York Central Railroad bridge on Seventh Street. He, along with the other men, described it as being a round and shiny looking thing with lights of several different colors. When they first saw it, the lights were orange, then turned a darker orange and white. They watched it travel very slowly southward and said it looked like it separated.

Mrs. Dolly Grady of 30th Street, said she had watched a similar UFO on Tuesday night for nearly an hour and said it had different colored lights.

We watched it for about 10 minutes.

AFB Claims 'UFO' Really Flying Boxcar

The "unidentified flying object" sighted Monday by a large number of Mason Countians has apparently been identified, although some are still not convinced.

According to the Gallipolis Daily Tribune, a spokesman for Lockbourne Air Force Base, near Columbus, said what area residents saw was a C-119 Flying Box Car on a training flight. The planes fly nightly over southeastern Ohio using what the spokesman described as "illuminator lights." The light is called the "Light of Freedom" and its use in Vietnam has been invaluable in revealing enemy position to American forces.

Repudiating this, two Point Pleasant youths said they "chased" the object seen Monday on motorcycles after noticing it hovering above the caretaker's building at Suncrest Cemetery and followed it out Sand Hill Road where they had it in sight about 20 minutes. They said because of the way it maneuvered they did not believe it to be a plane. Also, in some reports the object viewed was described as being round and not having any wings.

Area UFO Mystery Solved?

UFO-watching seems to have reached fever pitch in the past week as cars flock by the score to the TNT and Camp Conley area.

Thursday night, dozens of cars — some apparently carrying families on an outing — were parked in the TNT and along Route 62 near the Pleasant Point Resort. Many persons reported sighting an object with flashing lights traveling over the area around 8:30 p.m.

At the same time, three pilots for the Mason County Civil Defense unit followed what they believed to be the object.

Lou Mueller, Carl Sibley and Richard Newell said they followed the "object" to Huntington Tri-State Airport and discovered it was Allegheny Airlines flight 823.

They said the plane makes a daily flight from Washington, Philadelphia and Pittsburgh to Huntington and passes over Point Pleasant between 8:10 and 8:50 each evening, when on schedule.

The men said the plane is a twin-engine turbo-prop craft which makes no noticeable sound while in flight.

The plane also has a condenser lighting system on the nose, tail and back sides of both wingtips, which, they say, would explain the white flashing lights and red rotating beacons spotted by thousands in Mason County. The time of the flight was confirmed by Allegheny officials.

Last night, however, the object sighted here was also seen traveling north away from Huntington.

One former disbeliever who does not wish to be identified said a similar object followed her car while she and a friend were traveling along Sand Hill Road Wednesday night at 8:45 p.m. The object seemed to glide along slowly and at times came quite close to the car, she said. She described the object as being round and about seven feet in size. The lights on the object, she noted, were "the most beautiful red and white colors."

After losing sight of the object at Meadowbrook, she said, she drove to her home in Bellemeade where she again sighted the object just over some trees near her house.

Robert Wamsley of 400 First Street reports he has been sighting UFOs since December, usually between 8 and 9 p.m., but was most impressed by a sighting which he and about 12 others made Wednesday night over the river in Henderson.

Wamsley said they watched as three objects came together and hovered for a time. The objects split up when a jet plane flew over the area, he said.

'Flying Saucer' Nearly Has Its 'Wings' Clipped

One of the area's unidentified flying objects has been identified — and its "little green man" almost became a "little red-faced man."

A reliable spokesman said he witnessed the object in the sky, along with several others, this week and was almost convinced he had at last seen a UFO.

"I was sure it was an air-

plane," he said, "but there wasn't any sound."

"It glided over the hilltop (along Route 2 south of Point Pleasant). It had red, white, orange and other colored lights, and had two beams shining down from the bottom of it.

"I watched and it disappeared over the hill, but then I saw it return.

"But this time it got too close to the hilltop and he had to cut his engines on."

It was, in fact, an airplane and probably one UFO which has frightened many women and children in the vicinity of Route 2.

"He must have had every light, even the cabin lights, in the plane on," the spokesman said, "and maybe then some."

A plane gliding along trees also gave the appearance it was disappearing and then reappearing and at times made it look like it was standing still.

The plane and its prankster pilot had been gliding back and forth across the river for several nights.

His noisy flight, however, almost was his last as he almost clipped a few trees with his "saucer."

"He who laughs last. . . ."

Girls Say Red Object Chased Them On Road

POINT PLEASANT — Two young girls driving from Hartford to Point Pleasant Thursday night about 10 p.m suddenly noticed a red object chasing them. First the red light was seen in front of their car, then in back of them.

They said they could not identify the object, but were frightened by it. As they traveled fast it would also go fast and when they slowed down it would do the same. When they reached Point Pleasant the light suddenly disappeared, the girls said.

Sunday night in the northern section of Point Pleasant several people saw two bright lights that were a different color than lights of a plane and traveling slowly and silently.

The first one went toward a red object in the sky that moved very slowly. When the bright-lighted object reached the area close to the red light they both quickly disappeared and immediately another bright object made a zig-zag performance before it too disappeared like the turning off of an electric light.

THE MESSENGER, Athens, Ohio — Monday, June 5, 1967 — Page 7

Sightings Reported In Point, New Haven

POINT PLEASANT — Four boys camping out Friday night were frightened when they saw an unidentied object which they believe was the "Monster."

The boys were camping out near Lewis Street in Point Pleasant. The object appeared about 3 a.m. Saturday. It looked to be six or seven feet tall and was a gray colored according to the boys.

The boys said after what sounded like some wings flopping three times, it disappeared.

The camping ended right then, as the boys returned to one of their homes and sat up until daylight, then went to their respective homes.

A New Haven woman who went outside to check on her dogs about 11 p.m. Thursday night along with a neighbor saw a bright object in the sky. A short distance from it was another unidentified object in colors of blue and white. The objects suddenly disappeared.

Pool To Open

POINT PLEASANT — Shawnee Swimming Pool will open Tuesday for the season sponsored by the Point Pleasant Kiwanis Club.

The pool has been re-decorated in bright colors by the Keyette and Key Club members.

No Opposition

HENDERSON — There will be no opposition in the city election here Tuesday unless there are write-in votes, as only one party has filed. Candidates for the Peoples Party are:

Frank Morrison, mayor; Dreama Aiker, recorder; and Carl Neal, Effie Roach, Robert Mayes, Alice Noe, and Fulton Spears, city council. The polls will open at 6:30 a.m. and close at 7:30 p.m. The election will be held at City Hall.

More UFO Sightings Reported

POINT PLEASANT — Sightings of unidentified flying objects, reported by many witnesses over the past several weeks, continued in the Point Pleasant area Friday night.

Several persons reported they saw a round object with bright ray of lights making a circle in the downtown area over Central School.

Other reports were received from the Sandy Heights Addition vicinity between 9:30 and 10 p.m. Witnesses said the object was rotating.

A similar UFO has been spotted in the Huntington area over the past several weeks.

Three Youths Describe Big Mystery Bird

POINT PLEASANT — It may not have been the monster that has been seen by several in Mason County in recent weeks, but it was a mighty big bird according to three Point Pleasant High School students who reported that they saw this "thing" Monday night as they were driving on Staffhouse Road near Route 62 at 9:15 p.m.

The boys, Steve Clark, Brerry Casto and Bill Flowers, said it flew along with their car and they saw its wings which had a five-foot span.

They said that it looked brown with white spots under its wings. They didn't see a head or feet, but estimated that it might have been nearly four or four and one-half feet tall.

The boys said it did not look like a man, but more like a bird, although like nothing they had seen before. It came at them suddenly, and went out of sight quickly, too. They went back to look for it, but did not see it again.

The first sighting of the creature was by Mr. and Mrs. Roger Scarberry and Mr. and Mrs. Steve Mallette in almost the same area around midnight Nov. 15. It was reportedly much larger than the bird seen Monday and also a different color.

It was later seen by Connie Carpenter, New Haven, and Tom Ury, Clarksburg, both of whom described it as a large creature with red eyes and a large wing span. It chased their cars at a high rate of speed, they said.

Sighting 1-9-67

More Reliable Information

UFO Reports Gain Credence

This is the fifth in a series of articles appearing in The Herald-Advertiser and The Herald-Dispatch on unidentified flying objects. Hupco Reporter Ron Hite has researched hundreds of reports of UFOs in the Tri-State and interviewed Air Force officials at Dayton.

By RON HITE

UFO reports were dismissed as only the work of pranksters for many years, but recently well-informed and respected citizens have reported strange objects hovering in the sky. The fact that more reliable persons have reported UFO's means deeper consideration must now be given to such reports.

One such well-informed person who reported a sighting was Weirton Attorney John Vujnovie.

According to Mr. Vujnovic, the sighting was made last October 7 — the night before the West Virginia University-Pitt football game.

He described his experience this way:

"My 10-year-old son and I were driving south on State Rt. 66 from Chester, W. Va. to Weirton. We spotted an object in th esky as we were leaving the racetrack at Chester.

"While driving toward New Cumberland, we saw a light come on hovering near a hillside. The light started coming toward the car and I guess my son was frightened and I slowed the car so that we were a good distance behind the object.

"The object had an outer circular light that glowed, but there was no sound at all. I stopped the car for a better look and the thing started coming down over the highway. I think it was about 400 feet in the air."

He reported that the object looked about 25-feet in diameter and was about five-feet high at the widest point.

"At one time, it looked as if there were windows in the craft and after it got past we could see a revolving light. The outer glow of the light made a fast flickering type of

(See THREE, Page 10)

 Other portion of clipping is missing.

Ohio Woman Says UFOs Killed 2 Cows

By United Press International

West-central Ohioans continued to report sighting unidentified flying objects Sunday, including a woman who excitedly phoned police to say one landed in a pasture and killed a couple of dozing cows.

UFO sightings were reported in six counties with descriptions varying from "orange-colored objects" to "grayish discs with red and bluish-green lights."

Patrolman Charles Conklin of the Greenfield Police Department said a "very excited" woman told him Sunday night an oblong object with blinking lights landed in a nearby Highland County field, killing two cows.

The county sheriff dispatched an airplane and several cruisers to the area, but a three-hour search turned up no UFO and no dead cattle.

"Her directions were only half-way reliable," Conklin said adding that she hung up before he could get her name or address.

Separate sightings of what was described as a huge oval of amber light with a bright white middle band were reported by Madison County sheriff's deputy Robert Hunter and state employe Roger Spencer.

The object was hovering over the north side of London, Ohio according to Hunter who saw it from the Madison County sheriff's office. Spencer claimed he saw the object while working on the north side of the community at the Bureau of Criminal Identification.

In Montgomery County, an officer took a black and white photograph of an object with red and green blinking lights which reportedly showed very fine details of the UFO. Officials, however, refused to release the photo until further investigations are conducted.

In a three-county area along Interstate 75 between Dayton and Cincinnati, the UFO's were described as "grayish discs with red and bluish-green lights."

"It continuously glowed," said Lt. Charles Jones of the Madison County Sheriff's office. "It was traveling very slow. Very, very slow. It would go dim and then brighten up. It was actually in the shape of a blimp."

Source unknown

Oct-5/67

Page 6 — THE MESSENGER, Athe

Lights Seen By Family Near Park

NELSONVILLE — Strange lights moving east and west Tuesday night and early Wednesday morning were observed by Clyde Shingler and members of his family from their home on US 33 near the Diamond Roadside Park.

They reported there was no sound from the lighted objects and they could only class them as unidentified flying objects. At one time the sound of a single jet plane could be heard for a short period, it was said.

The lights would move from east to west circling at what appeared to be a light in the sky then moving west to east. This movement continued from about 7 p.m Tuesday to 4 a.m. Wednesday, Shingler reported.

Page 2 — THE MESSENGER, Athens, Ohio — Wed., Sept. 18, 1968

UFO Makes Return Visits Over Mason; Probe Asked

POINT PLEASANT — What unidentified object is flying over Mason County at night?

That is the question today and some people believe there should be an investigation.

Monday night the sheriff's office received calls describing a low-flying "crippled plane."

Three teen-age boys saw an object in the TNT area and said that the object's white light focused on them was so bright they could not look at it. The "round object" was about 300 feet long.

One time it appeared over the hilltop on Jerrico Road. Witnesses reported it had long and short prongs.

In the same area there was an object flying first fast, then slow. It would hover, displaying green, red and white lights.

An estimated 500 persons saw the object during the night.

Timmie Clendenin and Johnny Love said they saw a bright light at Ordnance School when they went to investigate, it "took off." They chased it to Route 2.

No one who saw the object, detected any wings. Some persons heard a humming sound, similar to that of an airplane or helicopter.

One person said the object stayed above his car while he was traveling home from his job.

A Letart man reported that the object circled the area there for 35 minutes.

People on Thomas Ridge said it stayed for 30 minutes or more in that area and was circling the area using the extremely bright searchlight on the ground.

It was also seen in the Meadowbrook and 30th Street areas.

Many first thought it was a pilot in trouble, trying to find a place to land, but the Mason County airport was lighted. The object went over it several times.

One teen-ager said that he saw a "big thing" recently that he could not identify. He said he was in the TNT area. He turned a curve and on the bank was a creature about 6 feet tall. It was white and had red eyes. He said he stopped his car but the creature ran. Others have reported seeing similar creatures in the area.

It has been about two years since the unidentified objects first appeared in this area. Two Point Pleasant couples saw a creature in the TNT area that chased them by gliding over their car into the city limits of Point Pleasant. Since that time many UFO's have been seen in that area as well as other places in the vicinity.

FIRST SINCE AUG. 14

Local 1699, Ohio U.

Mason Countians See UFO; Light Too Bright To Look At

POINT PLEASANT—Everyone looked skyward Monday night as residents in the Meadowbrook Addition watched an unidentified flying object.

For more than a half hour, the object hovered over the residential section north of midtown, on Sand Hill Rd.

Flashing red lights and a single "very intense" clear light that shone down from the bottom of the low-flying "craft," and swept across the area.

Some of the witnesses to the night flight said the light was so intense they could not look directly at it.

The object was seen moving in a southerly direction, toward Huntington, about 10:45 p. m.

A year ago, Mason countians in the Camp Conley area, north of Point Pleasant, said they saw a UFO.

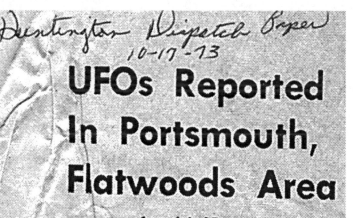

Huntington Dispatch Paper
10-17-73

UFOs Reported In Portsmouth, Flatwoods Area

Associated Press

PORTSMOUTH, Ohio — A Portsmouth radio newsman said he watched what he thought was an unidentified flying object for nearly three minutes last night in the skies over southern Ohio.

Dan Robbins of WPAY said the object appeared to be round and left a light, white trail in the sky as it sped away due east.

Robbins said a listener alerted him to the object at about 9:50 p.m.

Minutes earlier, Cincinnati police reported receiving numerous reports of UFO sightings.

At Ashland, Ky., radio station WCMI reported receiving about 25 calls from residents who claimed they had seen an UFO along Kentucky 207 in the Flatwoods area.

Law enforcement officials in the area said they had received no reports of sightings.

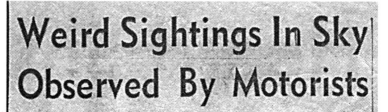

Weird Sightings In Sky Observed By Motorists

(Continued From Page 1)

third. "One of the lights was brighter than the other two," he said. He spotted the objects about 8:15 p. m.

His mother reported that she could also see the lights.

Two youths, Doug Martin, 13, of 145 Olive St. and Larry Roberts, 13, of 449 Linden Circle, another carrier boy, said they saw a reddish-green object moving in the direction of U. S. Rt. 60 about 8 p. m. on March 2.

They said the object looked as if it had about a dozen lights on the bottom which changed from white to yellow. The lights were also blinking in sequence.

Although some reports were received from the immediate area of Huntington, most of the sightings were in the Milton area.

The same night (March 2) as the sightings in Huntington, a Milton woman said she and a relative spotted a lighted object in the sky. She described the object as having at least three lights which gave off a yellow color and hovered low in the sky.

On Wednesday, March 1, about 9:30 p. m. another Milton woman said a strange, saucer-like object hovered over her car as she was driving home from church along U. S. Rt. 60.

She said the object moved slowly over her automobile at an altitude of 100 to 200 yards. She described it as being "round, flat on the bottom . . . dark, massive." It did not glow, she said, but it was well lighted. It had lights all around and on the left side were two blinking lights.

"I first noticed the object as I reached forward in the car to turn on the radio. It seemed the size of a small helicopter . . . maybe 20 feet or so in diameter." She emphasized that it could not have actually been a helicopter.

The following night a Wayne County man said he saw what appeared to be an object "made out of cloth, colored white and well lighted."

The object, he thought, was more oblong than round, but his two sons said they thought it was round. The object moved directly toward his car then veered upward and passed over them.

Among the other reports in the two-day period of March 2 and 3 there were reports that an International Nickel Co. employe saw a "strange bright white lights" about 2,000 feet above the ground hovering over the Twenty-ninth St. bridge at Rt. 60.

Also a Locust St. resident said his color television set suddenly went awry Wednesday night about 1 a. m. He said the colors on the screen scrambled and then the screen went black. He said he went into his yard to investigate the possible cause and saw a strange object passing through the sky. He also said a neighbor had reported the same incident.

Two teenagers reported that they saw a set of triangular shaped lights on both Thursday and Friday. They said they saw a total of four lights which were first white and then blinked red and white.

Source unknown; remainder missing

-Maybe Some Angels

By James A. Haught

Staff Writer

When Charleston becomes the temporary flying saucer capital of the world next week, related topics of attention may be "mothman," and a seer who says he communicates with "the space intelligences," and perhaps even two Mason Countians who believe they are angels.

About 75 UFO believers from all over the U.S. are expected to attend the sixth annual Congress of Scientific Ufologists June 20 and 21 in Charleston.

Most of the sessions will be held in privacy at the Daniel Boone Hotel, but a public meeting will be conducted at 7:30 p.m. June 21 in the Civic Center Little Theater.

* * *

ORGANIZERS OF THE congress point out that Theodore Owens of Philadelphia, a self-proclaimed mystical prophet ho claims to be in contact with "the ce intelligences," has predicted a t wave of flying saucer sightings weep the Charleston area before uring the congress.

h Jarrett of St. Albans, a Car- er and president of the UFO s society here, is to make ary speeches about the con- o appear before the Nation- nt Assn. at the American Nitro Thursday, and the Club at noon June 19.

Clarksburg, editor of a cer bulletin and author cer books, is chief or- gress. He said Charles- s a meeting place be- inia is such a good place cers."

* * *

E of UFO paydirt in the , Barker cited several ings here. He has gath- e sightings for a new ese examples:

merly of Dunbar, oper- liance store at Cross aw a strange, spherical r Cross Lanes the night of Jan. 19, 1967. Jones said the object was about 20 feet across, hovered above the pavement, then shot into the sky.

Barker said another driver—a Bancroft, Putnam County, man who doesn't want his name revealed—also saw the object the same night. He said the Bancroft man claims he was "buzzed by a water tank," a glowing cylinder that sped along I-64 and spurted over his truck.

►Woodrow Derenberger, formerly of Parkersburg, said that on the night of Nov. 2, 1966, a "dark hulk" descended in front of his van truck on I-77 near Parkersburg and forced him to stop. As the gray metallic object hovered over the pavement, he said, a man emerged from a door in it, walked to Derenberger's car and "talked" to him by extrasensory perception. The stranger said his name was "Cold" and that he came from "a country much less powerful than yours," Derenberger claimed. After the wordless chat, the visitor re-entered his craft and rose into the sky, he said.

►Another unidentified flying object listed in Barker's West Virginia tabulation is "mothman," a mysterious bird reported in various parts of the state for several years.

He says a Point Pleasant woman told him she first saw the creature on W.Va. 2 in 1961, describing it as man-sized and with "a set of huge wings that filled the entire width of the road." Also, she said, a bird-like thing "bumped" on the roof of her house and emitted "high-pitched beeping sounds" somewhat like electronic noises.

►The weirdest report in Barker's West Virginia list, however, concerns a Mason County man and wife who believe they are angels. He said they claim to be "in close contact with myriads of God's angels" and have been themselves turned into angels. Barker said they have built a jewelry-covered "scepter" with which they claim they can transmit signals to "between 5,000 and 7,000 angels" and keep them informed of earthly happenings.

Source unknown

Beulah Jones

'Around The Bend'

Point Pleasant Loses A Friend

Point Pleasant has lost a friend with the recent passing of Mary Hyre. It was her town and she knew every nook and cranny of it, making a permanent record of its progress and growth from a small, river town to one that made the front pages of the New York Times with the tragedy of the Silver Bridge.

Above all she respected the historical Americana of Point Pleasant and often recounted some of the exciting events in its past in her column "Where the Waters Mingle."

Mary Hyre enjoyed people and the close friendship that results when one lives in a small town where there are no secrets. She was helpful to others and they in turn, helped her in her work of reporting news.

She followed families and businesses in their joys and also their tragic moments. A fire in Point Pleasant wasn't just another fire, it represented a loss to the community.

She would have liked knowing the many friends who came to pay their respects, the beautiful flowers given in her memory, the final moments surrounded by family, co-workers, and friends. She was not alone.

Mary Hyre gave her best and that is the most one can do. Point Pleasant has a vacant place. But they will remember that she was the champion of the free word, and the right to "tell it like is was."

PART IV
CORRESPONDENCE & PERSONAL NOTES

Following are several letters from author John Keel (*The Mothman Prophecies*) to Linda Scarberry and her parents. Included in this section are some notes by Linda's mother Mabel regarding past historical sightings of a Mothman-like creature.

The authors wish to thank Ms. Scarberry and Mr. Keel for granting permission to reprint these personal letters.

John A. Keel

33RD STREET
NEW YORK 16, NEW YORK
MURRAY HILL

Dec. 20, 1966

Dear Everyone:

I have been very rushed since I returned to NYC Sat. night but I want to thank you for your many kindnesses during my visit to Pt. Pleasant ...I could never have accomplished anything without your help. I wish I could have stayed longer and been more effective in the situation.

The trip back to Washington was rather miserable. I ran into a bad snowstorm outside of Elkins and had to stay over there. Finally had to break down and buy a set of chains for the car.

I tried to interest the Pentagon in the Pt. Pleasant situation but they seemed quite unconcerned. Since no-one had officially complained to them about it, they chose to ignore it. Incidently, there is a UFO flap in Maryland at the moment...and the UFOs seem to have singled out specific people and are returning again and again.

After leaving Pt. Pleasant I thought of hundreds of things I should have checked. Perhaps later on I will send you a list of questions that you might be able to answer. Mary dropped me a Xmas card and enclosed a note saying you were going to send me some clippings. I'm looking forward to getting them.

Here is a copy of one of my newspaper stories. I have sent you a small package...something that might be useful to you.

Again, thanks for everything. I will keep in touch with you and let you know what I'm up to here.

Best...

John

---john a. keel

John A. Keel

33RD STREET
NEW YORK 16, NEW YORK
MURRAY HILL

February 14, 1967

Dear everyone:

I have been quite busy chasing UFOs here in the northeast but here are a couple of copies of the write-up which appeared recently in the bulletin of the Aerial Phenomena Research Organization in Tucson, Ariz. It is based upon clippings which I sent to them. I haven't had a chance to complete my lengthy report on the situation. The UFOs have been active all up and down the Ohio valley and are now very busy around Cairo, Ill. where the Ohio R. joins the Mississippi. Apparently they have been following the courses of our major rivers this past year.

Mrs. Hyre has written to me a couple of times and she passed along the terrible news of Brenda's husband's injuries in Viet Nam. I'm sorry and hope that he is recovering all right.

Connie and Kieth must be married now. I planned to send them a telegram but could not get through to Western Union...their blankety-blank phone is always busy. Anyway, give them my best when you see them.

Some of the editors at TRUE are very skeptical of the MOTHMAN and are presently debating the whole matter. But I think the story will go through and should be in print sometime this summer. I will send you a carbon copy of the final version, along with all the clips, etc. that I have collected. Perhaps Mary has shown you some of the material I have been sending her. Mothman was seen further south last Sept. before he decided to settle in Pt. Pleasant.

Again, I was very sorry to hear about Brenda's husband.

Drop me a note when you have the time and let me know what is happening.

Best... John A. Keel

---john a. keel

John A. Keel

[redacted]
P. O. Murray Hill Station
New York, N. Y. 10016

Sept. 24, 1968

Dear Parke and Mabel;

Thanks for the two letters and the clipping. The fall "flap" is well underway. The reports are coming in from all over. Thus far nothing really serious has happened but our funny friends are sure kicking up a fuss. Haven't heard from Mary since Gray's "convention". That turned out as I expected. Moseley and his friends came back to NYC convinced that it was all "mass hysteria" inspired by Mary's newspaper accounts. They admitted they didn't talk to anybody except Millard Halstead and a bus boy at the Resort. Mary apparently told them about some of the things her relatives had seen and they (Tim Beckeley and Moseley) told me they suspected Mary was making it all up or something. I do wish she had heeded my advice and been more cautious around those characters.

Some months back I was told to expect a visit from a man carrying a bible. This may have been the odd fellow who appeared around Mary's office. I kid you not when I say that "they" are trying to lure me back to W. Va. again. I suppose they would love to get their hands on me...after all the stuff I've been writing.

An exceptionally tall "prowler" is also busy in New York state. Has bushy hair and a strange laugh. He's been popping up around isolated farms. There have been a rash of mysterious fires in the area, animals disappearing, etc. All the farmers are scared to death. Canada has also been having a big flap and there have been some very strange incidents up there. Whoever they are, whereever they're from, they are now here in large numbers and only a handful of us are trying to cope with this wild situation.

I don't think Linda and Roger will have any problems in Cleveland but let me know if they do. Perhaps we can expect something a bit more spectacular than usual...designed to get me scurrying back down there.

I have finished moving and am now trying to unpack and sort out all of my junk, papers, etc. It has been a very big job and has taken up most of my time this month.

Hope you are all okay. The invisible characters are playful but harmless <u>unless</u> you smell a very strong odor of some kind. Don't let 'em upset you. They feed on fear. If you panic, they get much worse. If you have a very strong feeling that someone is around...try talking to them. Tell them very firmly that you know they are there and you wish they would go away. (I know this sounds insane so please don't repeat it to "outsiders". They'll think we're all nuts.)

Now there's one more thing I want you to try. The next time you hear a thud against the side of the house, talk to it. Tell "it" to

-2

answer with one thump for "YES" and two thumps for "NO". Then ask it questions such as : "Do you know that Dani is gone?" "Are we in danger?" etc. Let me know all the details if this should happen. People in other places have been able to do this.

Since "they" have been around Pt. Pleasant for two years now it looks as if they mean to stay. It's time for us to try to communicate with them there if we can. Keep in touch with Mrs. Thomas. It's a good bet that she will eventually be contacted in some direct manner.

Keep me posted and I'll write whenever I can. Maybe I'll try to call Mary again soon.

All the best...

-john a. keel

February 4, 1970

Dear Linda and all;

I received your first letter last Saturday and your second one xxxxx yesterday. I sent Mary a get-well card and note last week after talking to you. She has probably rewieved it by now.

I won't try to call her just now. It sounds as if she is suffering the classic post-coronary depression and I'm sure her doctors have had experience with this and will be working to pull her around. They're probably keeping her heavily doped up and this adds to her lethargy. In a few days she will snap back to her old self. It is a terrible trauma to find yourself facing death and uncertainty about life. A ne call from me at this point might even be detrimental, particularly she feels some kind of strain...some urge to tell me something. could trigger another attack. If I call when she is filled with ugs, she might not even remember the call anyway and so it would complish nothing...and might even do harm.

Mary has been bothered by a lot of cranks and weirdos and she has pparently taken some of them seriously. My own life is threatened y some nut about once a week. If I took them seriously I would have een in the booby hatch long ago. When such threats fail, "they" often ake to issuing threats to people who know me. I get mail all the time rom people all over the country who are concerned because they have received such threats and warnings. Maybe they've been playing this game with Mary more than you know about.

She is made of stern stuff and if the doctors can keep her put for awhile she will certainly pull through. But I fear her working days might be over and retirement would be very hard for her to take. We can only hope that things are not as bad as they seem right now. When she is feeling a little better I will try to call her.

I hope you haven't set off a wave of rumors in the hospital. Rumors that will soon spread all over Ohio and W. Va. There are a lot of screwballs who think that Mary and I invented the whole Mothman thing just to have something to write about!

Recently Dr. Jacques Vallee published a book titled "Passport to Magonia" and he mentioned Mabel in it. I will try to make and enclose a photostat copy of that page.

My two forthcoming books will deal at length with Mothman and the UFO sightings around Point Pleasant. One will be out in April in paperback and will probably be on sale in Pt. Pleasant. The other will be a hardcover and will appear in June. Gray Barker has written a book called "The Silver Bridge" and it should be out soon. Probably filled with a lot of crap but who knows?

There isn't much chance that I will be able to get down to W. Va. in the near future. I seem to be having troubles from every quarter. Hope you are all well. Please keep me informed of Mary's progress.

Best...

-john a. keel

Feb. 20, 1970

Dear Mabel, Parke, Linda and all;

I have been frantically trying to call W. Va. all week without success. I can get nothing but a busy signal at your number. I also tried to call Mary's house and office and got no answer at all.

Dan came by on Monday to tell me the terrible news. I have not even been able to reach him by phone since then.

It seems as if I spent hours in pay phones this week, cursing Alexander Graham Bell and all his descendents. The phone situation here is really ridiculous. When I first tried to call you on Monday night I could not even get a line through to W. Va.!

Even though things are very tight for me financially at the moment I wanted to somehow get down to Point Pleasant for the funeral. But I couldn't reach anyone to find out when the funeral was going to take place.

When you get a chance I hope you will be able to write and send me all the details, clippings, etc. Frankly, I expected Mary to pull through this so I was doubly shocked when Dan came by. I wish there was something I could have done. I feel so helpless and frustrated sitting here without a phone, quite cut off from everything.

I will keep trying to call you and maybe I will reach you before you get this letter. I tried to call you again a few minutes ago. Maybe somebody somewhere doesn't want me to return to W. Va.

Unhappily;

-john a. keel

March 15, 1970

Dear Mabel, Linda and Parke;

Several people in the Ohio valley have written to me to tell me about Mary. I wish I could have gotten to Point Pleasant for the funeral but it simply wasn't possible and everything seemed to work to interfere. I still can't quite believe she is gone. We had a lot of strange experiences together which we never told anyone about. But she never pried or asked questions. She just listened quietly. When she was in New York last spring she seemed pale and a little disspirited. I urged her to go into semi-retirement but I knew she wouldn't.

Now my two books are finished and will be out soon. Both of them mention Mary and describe some of the events in Pt. Pleasant. I will try to send you copies as soon as they are available. When the books come out you are apt to be bothered by a new collection of weirdos, cranks and teen-aged UFO buffs. But W. Va.'s Mothman is now a part of history, like the Flatwoods monster of 1952. In time it will become a folk legend.

The collapse of the Silver Bridge also had special meaning to me. You will be surprised when you read about it in my book, OPERATION TROJAN HORSE. There was so much going in Pt. Pleasant that no-one knew about...except Mary and myself.

I hope you are all well and that things are going all right for you. I owe Ake Franzen a letter and will try to write to him this week. Do you hear from him regularly?

All the best... John

-john a. keel

Parts of a letter received from John A. Keel, N.Y., written 1-2-67:

The situation in Pt. Pleasant seems to be quite complex. UFO activity began in the northern stretches of the Ohio River in March, 1966 and slowly continued along the river until late fall. Pt. Pleasant is just one of many spots being closely scrutinized by "who-knows-what." But it is a microcosm which may furnish us with important clues that will point to a final solution of the mystery.

Here's what to look for in your wanderings:

1.– Deposits of metalic substances such as strips of metal foil or piles of ordinary slag. This stuff will appear suddenly in farm fields, etc. In some instances,

MABEL McDANIEL 1

This letter is a hand-written copy of another letter from John Keel to Linda Scarberry; Linda's mother, Mabel McDaniel, made this copy.

— *Transcription by Lori Sergent*

Parts of a letter received from John A. Keel, N.Y. , written 1-2-67:

The situation in Pt. Pleasant seems to be quite complex. UFO activity began in the northern stretches of the Ohio River in March, 1966 and slowly continued along the river until late fall. Pt. Pleasant is just one of many spots being closely scrutinized by "who-knows-what." But it is a microcosm which may furnish us with important clues that will point to a final solution of the mystery.

Here's what to look for in your wanderings:

1.—Deposits of metalic substances such as strips of metal foil or piles of ordinary slag. This stuff will appear suddenly in farm fields, etc. In some instances, . . .

2/ People will tell you that they have seen such substances being discharged by low-flying UFOs. If any of these things do turn up, send me samples if you can.

2— If you get a UFO landing report, measure the holes left in the ground and look for deposits of a jelly-like liquid. Collect this liquid in bottles, using sticks in chop-stick fashion to pick it up. (It may burn your fingers.) Also look for burned foliage and for freshly dug earth. The latter will appear in perfect circles. If ~~these~~ you dig down a few feet you may find one or more small round metal spheres. If these spheres turn up, ship

2/

. . . people will tell you that they
have seen such substances being
discharged by low-flying UFOs. If
any of these things do turn up,
send me some samples if you can.

2.— If you get a UFO landing report,
measure the holes left in the ground
and look for deposits of a jelly-
like liquid. Collect this liquid in
bottles, using sticks in chop-
stick fashion to pick it up. (It
may burn your fingers.) Also
look for burned foilage [sic] *and for*
freshly dug earth. The latter will
appear in perfect circles. If
you dig down a few feet
you may find onc or morc
small round metal spheres.
If these spheres turn up, ship. . .

3/ one to me Collect. Do Not Give Them To The Air Force or To Local Authorities who may Turn Them over To The Air Force. Handle the spheres with gloves.

3.– Keep on the lookout for stories of stolen dogs or cattle.

4.– Let me know if any strangers appear in Pt. Pleasant and threaten any of the witnesses in any way. Try to get a complete description of such strangers -- how they are dressed, what kind of car they are driving and license plates.

5.– You may soon start getting peculiar stories of luminous globs of red or white light appearing in houses. Watch for them.

3/

. . . one to me collect. <u>Do Not Give Them To The Air Force or To Local Authorities Who May Turn Them Over To The Air Force</u>. Handle the spheres with gloves.

3.—Keep on the lookout for stories of stolen dogs or cattle.

4.—Let me know if any strangers appear in Pt. Pleasant and threaten any of the witnesses in any way. Try to get a complete description of such strangers—how they are dressed, what kind of car they are driving and license plates.

5.—You may soon start getting peculiar stories of luminous globs of red or white light appearing in houses. <u>Watch for them.</u>

-4-

6.– Watch for "Peeping Tom" reports, particularly if the peeper is described as "a very large man."

7.– Pay attention to all far-out stories – for instance: if a woman tells you that she had a dream in which she saw a little man standing in front of the crib of her baby, find out the date of the "dream" and obtain the racial background of the family.

8.– Try to obtain Doctors statements concerning persons being physically affected from "sightings".

It would prove worthwhile to keep a simple (brief facts) notebook on these things, recording only the

-4-

6.—Watch for "Peeping Tom" reports, particularly if the peeper is described as a "very large man."

7.—Pay attention to all far-out stories—for instance: if a woman tells you that she had a dream in which she saw a little man standing in front of the crib of her baby, find out the date of the "dream" and obtain the racial backround of the family.

8.—Try to obtain Doctors statements concerning persons being physically affected from "sightings."

It would prove worthwhile to keep a simple (brief facts) notebook on these things, recording only the. . .

-5-

dates, names and addresses of witnesses, and a very brief description of the incident. Eventually you will find a pattern developing, even with the wildest stories.

I would like to know what kind of waste chemicals the Pantasote Plant is dumping into the Ohio River and how often they dump chemicals there. This could be an important lead.

also am interested in knowing if the Experimental Farm uses any form of radioactive isotopes in their work or any special chemicals.

J.A.K."

-5-

. . . dates, names and addresses of witnesses, and a very brief description of the incident. Eventually you will find a pattern developing, even with the wildest stories.

I would like to know what kind of waste chemicals the Pantasote Plant is dumping into the Ohio River and how often they dump chemicals there. This could be an important lead.

Also am interested in knowing if the Experimental Farm uses any form of radioactive isotopes in their work or any special chemicals.

J.A.K.

-1- Historical Sightings
of Creature or Winged Man.

1- Sept. 18th 1877 - Winged human form
Sighted over Brooklyn, NY.

2 - 1915 thru 1917 - Witnesses Saw
White, Winged human form in the
Skies over Portugal - was described
as headless and was assumed by
Some as a religious Vision.

3 - Oct. 3 - 1917 - "The Miracle of Fatima"..
Huge silverly disc decended through
clouds of 70,000 people. Many had
cameras - Took pictures - Nothing
showed on film - - Religious interpretation.

4 - 1922 - Two witnesses in
Nebraska saw a Circular flying
craft land. In both cases, Tall
Winged Creatures were said To
have disembarked and flew away.

(Con't)

MABEL McDANIEL 2

These notes on "Winged-Man" sightings were made by Linda's mother, Mabel McDaniel.

— *Transcription by Lori Sergent*

-1-

Historical Sightings of Creature or Winged Man

1.—Sept. 18th 1877—Winged human form sighted over Brooklyn, NY.

2.—1915 thru 1917—Witnesses saw white, winged human form in the skies over Portugal—was described as headless and was assumed by some as a religious vision.

3.—Oct. 3 - 1917—" The Miracle of Fatima". . . Huge silvery disc decended through clouds of 70,000 people. Many had cameras—Took pictures—nothing showed on film—Religious interpretation.

4.—1922—Two witnesses in Nebraska saw a circular flying craft land. In both cases, tall winged creatures were said to have disembarked and flew away.

-2-

One witness was a hunter, The other a scientist from the University of Nebraska.

5 — Nov. 22, 1963 - Kent, England - four young people saw a luminous oval land in a field nearby and a tall, headless figure with wings shuffled out of it. and approached them.... they fled. Later, giant foot prints were found in that Area and reports of seeing a pulsating light in the sky.

6 — 1966 - Morristown, N.J. - A giant headless Creature frightened several witnesses in wooded Area of Historical Park. It moved awkwardly. No wings were reported, but sightings bear some resemblance to descriptions in Pt. Pleasant case.

-2-

*One witness was a hunter,
the other a scientist from The
University of Nebraska.*

*5.—Nov. 22, 1963—Kent, England—four
young people saw a luminous
oval land in a field nearby and
a tall, headless figure with wings
shuffled out of it and approached
them—they fled. Later, giant
foot prints were found in
that area and reports of seeing
a pulsating light in the sky.*

*6.—1966—Morristown, N.J.—A giant
headless creature frightened
several witnesses in wooded
area of Historical Park. It
moved awkwardly. No wings
were reported, but sightings bear
some resemblance to descriptions
in Pt. Pleasant case.*

-3-

7- July, 1966 - Saucer Sightings in Lost Creek, W.Va _ directly North of Flatwoods - 85 miles Northeast of Point Pleasant.

8- Flatwoods, W.Va. - 1952 - Monster sighted - giant Creature with rays of light blazing from its eyes. Witnesses were ill afterwards --- Vomiting and suffering from eye trouble. Creature has been seen periodically in the area since Then.

Flatwoods is approximately 70 miles directly east of Pt. Pleasant.

Nov. 15 - 1966 - Four persons were chased by a winged Creature at The speed of 100-105 mph. Creature was described as being app. 6 foot tall, with a

-3-

7.—July, 1966—Saucer sightings in Lost Creek, W. Va.—directly North of Flatwoods—85 miles Northeast of Point Pleasant.

8.—Flatwoods, W.Va.—1952—Monster sighted—giant creature with rays of light blazing from its eyes. Witnesses were ill afterwards—Vomiting and suffering from eye trouble. Creature has been seen periodically in the area since then. Flatwoods is approximately 70 miles directly east of Point Pleasant.

Nov. 15—1966—Four persons were chased by winged creature at the speed of 100-105 mph. Creature was described as being app. 6 foot tall, with a. . .

-4-

10 foot wing span. Eyes of blazing red, 2 inches in diameter and app. 6 inches apart, having a hypnotizing effect on witnesses. Creature had trunk & body form of human being. Was light gray & brown in color. On Nov. 27-66, [redacted] [redacted] also saw same creature in daylight. Creature has been seen periodically in the area since then. Some witnesses have been physically affected after sightings. Many saucer sightings have been reported during December of 1966, along Ohio River.

FROM- MRS. MABEL McDANIEL.

- 4 -

. . . 10 foot wing span. Eyes of blazing red, 2 inches in diameter and app. 6 inches apart, having a hypnotizing effect on witnesses. Creature had trunk & body form of human being. Was light gray & brown in color. On Nov. 27 – 66, [Eyewitness #8] also saw same creature in daylight. Creature has been seen periodically in the area since then. Some witnesses have been physically affected after sightings. Many saucer sightings have been reported during December of 1966, along the Ohio River.

From—Mrs. Mabel McDaniel.

APPENDICES

Appendix 1: Return to TNT—Part 1

Photos by Daniel Carter

These photographs (pages 156-158) of the abandoned North Power Plant, from the personal collection of Daniel Carter, were taken during a promotional photo shoot for a local band.

The date is circa 1990. All the mechanical systems (boilers, smokestacks, turbines, etc.) had been stripped out by this time, leaving just the empty shell—subsequently torn down just a few years later.

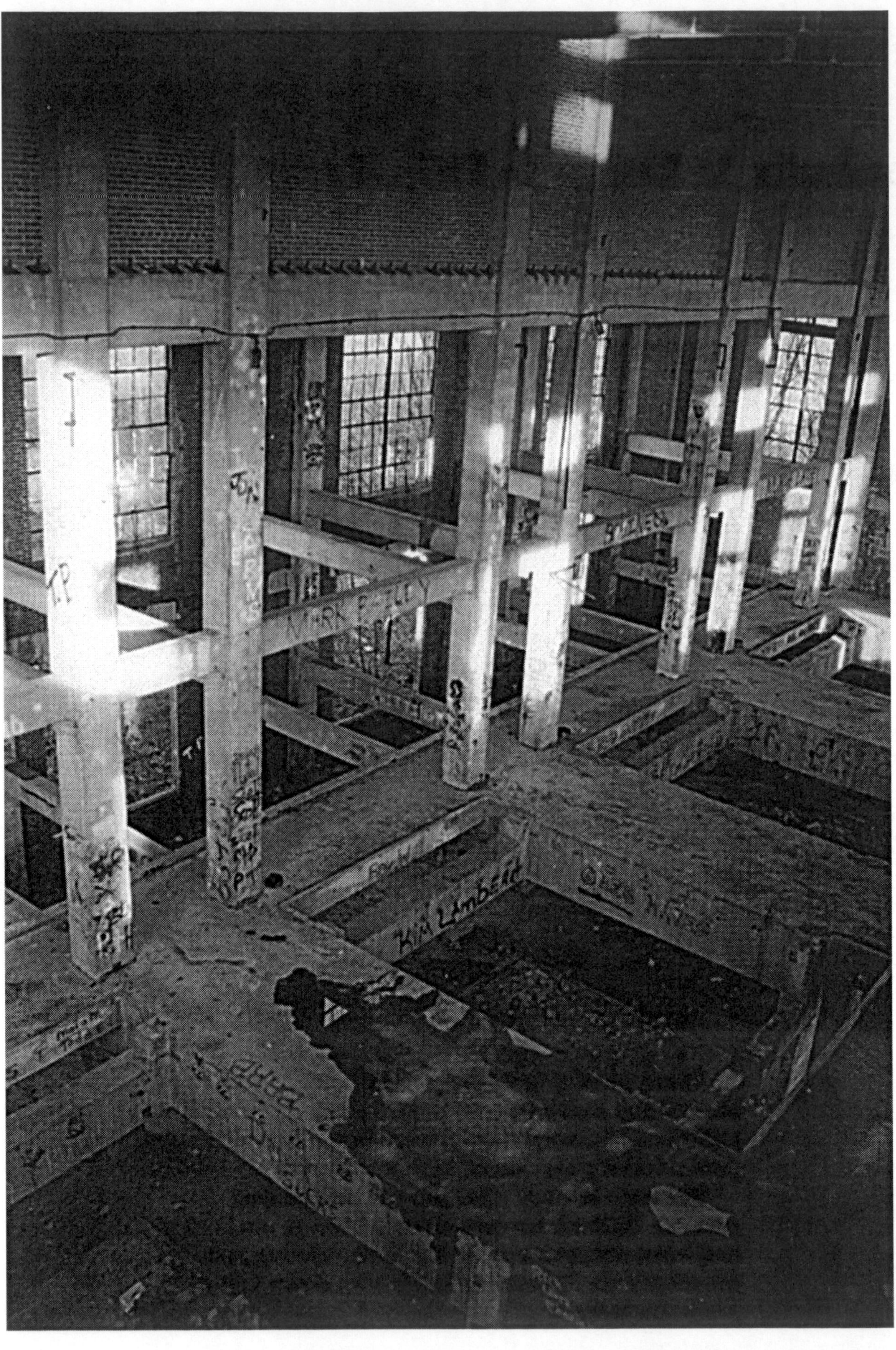

Appendix 2: Return to TNT—Part 2

Photos by Dani Scarberry

Linda Scarberry standing by the gate adjacent to where the North Power Plant once stood.

David Grabias, producer of documentary films for such notable organizations as National Geographic, The Discovery Channel, The Sci-Fi Channel, and others, contacted us during the summer of 2001 about filming a segment in the TNT area. He and employees of his company, Sinema Productions of Los Angeles, California, were going to be in Point Pleasant to film a documentary about the Mothman legend for the Sci-Fi Channel and USA Network. The finished product was created to generate interest for the Sony Pictures' film, "The Mothman Prophecies," due out in early 2002.

On September 12, 2001, Linda Scarberry agreed to ride up the TNT area with us and retrace the original route that she and the other three people in the car took on the night of November 15, 1966. It was an informative trip that answered many of our questions about the first Mothman sighting in the Point Pleasant, West Virginia, area. David graciously allowed us to take a few behind-the-scenes pictures of the production to include in this book.

We began our trip from the lower end of Point Pleasant and drove north on State Route 62. The documentary film crew followed us as we journeyed toward the TNT area. As we approached the Mason County Fairgrounds, Linda had us turn onto a gravel road. She began telling us about when she learned how to drag race on a stretch of paved road in the TNT area alongside more experienced drivers.

In the time leading up to November, 1966, people came from miles around to show off their

Linda Scarberry re-tracing the route the car traveled when she first sighted the Mothman on the evening of November 15, 1966.

muscle cars and their driving skills. This, of course, was not something the local law enforcement was happy about, and many chases occurred as a result. Linda said, "The racers came from as far as Middleport, Ohio, Pomeroy, Ohio, Ripley, West Virginia, Ravenswood, West Virginia, and, of course, Point Pleasant, West Virginia."

As we approached the long stretch of road that leads to the vacant lot that once housed the north power plant, Linda explained how, in 1966, the area was not yet overgrown with hedges and trees as it is today. She told us it was an area that was well-kept and the tall grass and weeds were almost non-existent at that time. The documentary crew began filming at this moment and had her repeat this statement, and continue talking about her experience.

The on camera interview begins with Linda explaining where and how the first sighting occurred.

One item that sparked our curiosity was the direction in which the two couples drove towards the north power plant the night the sighting occurred. Most people are familiar with the side road leading north to where the plant stood, adjacent to the Mason County Fairgrounds. Linda explained that they drove to the north power plant area from behind the Fairgrounds, north to south, from a different access road into the TNT area. After seeing the creature, they exited onto the main road in front of the Fairgrounds.

Both power plants (the north plant had a twin, the south power plant on the other side of Fairgrounds Road) were demolished in the early 1990s. As we looked into the fenced vacant lot, Linda pointed to the spot where they first caught a glimpse of Mothman, and told us how it quickly darted into the large building. She explained

Sinema Productions setting up for the on camera interview with Linda Scarberry. Center of photo shows Linda Scarberry, authors Donnie Sergent Jr. and Jeff Wamsley. Standing at far-right is producer David Grabias.

that as the group came over the small hill in the road, the first thing that caught her eye was a cable bouncing up and down—caused by the creature attempting to free itself from the cable near a fence surrounding the power plant.

As we drove out of the TNT area, we began to re-trace the direction the couples drove that night after realizing they were being followed by the Mothman. Once we turned back onto State Route 62, Linda pointed to the left of the road. She said a large billboard once stood there and this is where they witnessed the creature fly straight up into the air and then begin to follow the car as they drove toward Point Pleasant at speeds over 100 mph.

When we approached what is now the current location of the National Guard Armory, Linda told us that as she looked out the window of their car back in 1966 she could see that the Mothman was almost gliding through the air—flapping its wings almost effortlessly as it wove back and forth just above the car. Linda told us the wingspan was so large that the wings were hitting the side of the doors on the car as they sped down the highway. Later that night they discovered the paint scratched away on the side door panels of the black 1957 Chevy.

The film crew changes angles for another on camera interview. Just across the fence is where the North Power Plant stood during the sighting in 1966.

As we neared Point Pleasant she pointed to where they had seen the large, dead dog laying on the right side of the road on their way up to the TNT area earlier. Upon returning later that November evening, the dog was gone.

We continued our drive back through town while Linda reminisced about the week of the

Mothman sightings and how the town of Point Pleasant has changed since those days. She gave us detailed accounts of her experiences of the days following the couple's encounter. (These experiences are covered in the "Interview" section of this book.)

The TNT trip that day was a step back into history for everyone present and served as a firsthand account for all the events that occurred on November 15, 1966.

Appendix 3: Additional Resources

Books/CD-Roms

Keel, John. *The Mothman Prophecies.* Tor Books, 2007. Featuring a new cover, the book came back in print in early 2007. Sony Pictures used this book as a basis for its 2002 motion picture of the same name starring Richard Gere.

Mothman: The Facts Behind the Legend CD-ROM. 2002. Includes color photos, screen saver, video footage, audio clips and more. Check availability at www.mothmancasebook.com.

Tourism Websites

www.callwva.com — the official tourism website of West Virginia

www.masoncountytourism.org — the official tourism website of Mason County, West Virginia

www.pointpleasantwv.org — the official website for information about Point Pleasant, West Virginia

www.mothmanmuseum.com — the official website of "The World's Only Mothman Museum" in downtown Point Pleasant, West Virginia

Additional Websites

www.mothmanlives.com — a regularly updated website about Mothman and Point Pleasant, West Virginia; features annual Mothman festival information; offers Mothman merchandise

www.mothmancasebook.com — another regularly updated website about Mothman and Point Pleasant, West Virginia; features podcasts and information; offers Mothman merchandise

Acknowledgments

Donnie Sergent, Jr.
Point Pleasant, West Virginia native

I would like to thank my Lord and Savior Jesus Christ for His guidance, my mother Shirley for teaching me the importance of hard work and honesty, my father Donnie Sr. for teaching me the importance of patience and the golden rule, and for introducing me to the outdoor world at an early age, including fishing, hunting, camping, and the extreme importance of firearm safety, my wife Lori for being my best friend and supporting my decisions on my many endeavors, my grandfather Leonard and grandmother Lelah for keeping the Lord's words in my life, John Keel, David Grabias, Susan Rued, Mark Phillips for the book layout, all the employees at all Criminal Records store locations for never letting me have a dull day while working on my laptop, my best friends Joe Shinn and Paul Wroten for being the TNT fishing partners that they are, and my friend Jeff for allowing me to prove that I could use my computer for something more than playing hard drive-hogging adventure games. The support these people have given me in my effort to release this book and create the Mothmanlives.com website has been great. Without any of these folks, this book would still be on the hard drive of my laptop. I would also like to thank *everyone* who has supported the website and my efforts to bring tourism interest and business back to my hometown of Point Pleasant, WV and surrounding areas, including the guys and girls at the Speedway on Jackson Pike in OH, who always bring a smile to my face in the morning and supply me with coffee to get my day started. Thanks to YOU, who bought this book and are reading it, right now. Stop by and visit us at Point Pleasant, you are welcome, anytime.

Jeff Wamsley
Point Pleasant, West Virginia native

Thanks to God, my wife Julie and daughter Ashley, my mother Doris Wamsley and my late father Charles Dale Wamsley for all their love and support, my sister Joee Simpson, Mike, Haley and Katey Simpson, Wally Fetty, Donnie Sergent Jr. for a great and fun project, all the loyal customers who supported Criminal Records, Linda Scarberry and family, John Keel, David Grabias, Susan Rued, Mark Phillips, Charlie Cline, Jeremy Pitchford, Scott Short, Butch and Bernie from Kittaning Foodland. To all of you and those I may have forgotten to mention, I thank you for truly making my dreams come true.

CPSIA information can be obtained at www.ICGtesting.com
Printed in the USA
BVOW05s1507100813

328325BV00003B/23/A

9 780966 724677